Gue   n the West

Lessons for the West
From a Lifetime in the East

Hugh MacMahon

ORIGINAL WRITING

ISBNS
Parent : 978-1-78237-849-5
epub: 978-1-78237-850-1
mobi: 978-1-78237-851-8
PDF: 978-1-78237-852-5

A cip catalogue for this book is available from the National Library.

Published by Original Writing Ltd., Dublin, 2015.
Printed by Clondalkin Group, Glasnevin, Dublin 11

My thanks to the people in Korea and China who welcomed me as a guest and led me to appreciate an alternative approach to life.

Also, to my confreres Colm McKeating and Michael Molloy, and also to Karen Whelan and Steven Hope, for their suggestions.

Contents

Foreword

In June 1961, when Ireland celebrated the 1,500th anniversary of the death of St Patrick, it was the most impressive national religious event between the 1932 Eucharistic Congress and the visit of Pope John Paul ll in September 1979.

For the Patrician Year over two hundred church dignitaries came from around the world, led by the Papal Legate, Cardinal Gregoire Agagianian. Vampire jets of the Air Corp escorted the Cardinal's plane into Irish airspace and he was met at the airport by the Taoiseach and leading politicians. 100,000 people lined his route to Aras an Uachtarain. The Cardinal, besides being the head of the Vatican Department for Missions, was an Armenian Patriarch and with his bearded face and red headdress, draped back in Oriental style, he added an exotic element.

One of his duties in Dublin was to bless the foundation stone of a 60-foot statue of the Virgin Mary in Dublin Dockland. It cost £60,000, half of which was contributed by Dublin Dockers. The possibility that the Church's role in Ireland would be profoundly diminished within people's lifetime crossed no one's mind.

To mark that occasion in 1961, a series of talks on the legacy of St Patrick and the future of the Irish Church was held in the National Stadium in Dublin. The presentations were made from the boxing ring. Few paid as much attention to the words of one of the speakers, Tim Connolly, as I did. He was head of the Maynooth Mission to China, now better known as the Columban Fathers, of which I was a student member. He ended his talk on the Irish missionary tradition by saying, 'Seven years ago our last missionary was expelled from China but we look forward to the day when that country is open once more to the outside world. We believe that China has much to offer society and religion in the West.'

Considering the anti-China, anti-Mao and 'Yellow Peril' hysteria of that time, his statement was unexpected. It was not long since two of his priests had been killed in China and fifteen finally released from years in prison, so the idea that China might have something valuable to offer the Western world was as hard to appreciate as Mao himself.

Perhaps the Church in Ireland had something to learn from the Vatican but the suggestion that an alien and unchristian country like China had something to teach the 'Isle of Saints and Scholars' was hard to take seriously.

I was probably one of the few who took Tim's words at face value and they stayed with me in Asia where I was to spend more than half my life exploring what the Orient had to offer. In 2012 I returned to an Ireland that was almost a reversal of 1961.

A symbol of the new Dublin was the reconstructed Docklands where the Irish Missionary Union, in which I worked, was located. The Patrician Year's 60-foot statue of Our Lady had finally been erected in 1972 but the docks themselves were a thing of the past with roll-on, roll-off ferries and container freight making them obsolete. IT companies and modern town houses had replaced them. Social attitudes had just as dramatically been transformed.

Unlike the Docklands the Catholic Church had been less successful in reconstructing itself. National celebrations would no longer be of a religious nature, the clerical image was tarnished by scandals and many Church institutions seemed outdated. Missionary Societies had no new applicants for almost fifteen years.

If ever there was a time when Western society and religion could do with inspiration from outside this was it. It could be expected that those who had spent years abroad might draw on their experiences while living as long-term guests in Asia, Africa and Latin America and come forward with alternative approaches and a fresh vision. However, the missionaries were subdued.

They had never been encouraged, or trained, to reflect on what they had learnt in another culture and apply it to their home country. Enormous changes had questioned their self-identity and they still had to understand why.

Two challenges in particular faced them.

First, they needed to pause and consider what they had gathered from their encounter with other cultures. Where did the positive response they had received, the mind-broadening alternative world-views they had experienced and the joyful celebrations that had energised them spring from? Only when they fully understood the sources of what had changed them could they begin to find ways of sharing that enthusiasm back home.

Second, they had to face up to the reasons why the Irish missionary movement with its 1,500 year tradition was now in danger of fading into history. In future, who would bring back fresh ideas and inspiration gained from long-term participation in another culture?

Fresh from Asia, and with Tim Connolly's challenge still on my mind, I began tracing the slow process and small events in which I myself had been challenged by the people I met and the places I lived, how I had learnt to think differently and what that might have to offer people back home.

Chapter 1
Fresh from the West

The Chinese claim it was their 'Old Master,' Lao Tzu, who first said a journey of a thousand *li* begins with one step. I got the push to take that initial step, not in my native Ireland or in China where I was to spend many years later, but in a village deep in the rice fields of Cholla Province, South Korea. And the unlikely person to give me the shove was an American Air Force sergeant.

With just six months of language study behind me, I was temporarily in charge of the country parish of Kanjin. It was not a taxing assignment. The local Catholics appeared at 5.45 am for Mass, in Latin, and even if I was able to converse with them they were in a hurry back to their fields. For the rest of the day I was free. In 1964 the country was still recovering from three years of devastating war and getting life back to normal was everyone's priority. There were no young people with time on their hands to chat with a foreigner who would be there only three weeks and spoke virtually no Korean.

Most of the church-goers lived in thatched houses behind tall stucco walls in the nearby village. Their tile-roofed gateways suggested a desire for privacy and there were no invitations to visit. Fortunately our mission training included lengthy periods of monastic silence which helped prepare us for such isolation.

The only person, besides the Mass-goers, whom I met on a regular basis was the cook, an elderly lady with absolutely no English who appeared at meal time and disappeared soon afterwards. She gave impetus to my on-going language studies by regularly forcing me to thumb through my dictionary for essential words such as 'hot water,' 'spoon' and 'soap.'

As a result I was only too happy to hear that the American Sisters who ran a girls school nearby were expecting visitors and wanted me to provide them with accommodation. The guests were two US Air Force sergeants, neighbours of the Sisters back in the States, and based at Kunsan airfield. Because of the distance involved the visitors had to stay overnight.

I was expecting them around 3.00 pm and on the hour I went out into the yard which was still steaming from the last monsoon shower. I had a long wait. The unpaved road from Kunsan rambled from one nameless village to another and if there were any signs for Kangjin they would be in Korean or, worse still, Chinese characters. I began to doubt whether the soldiers' map-reading skills were up to it.

At 5.00 pm, as the electricity was about to come on, I heard the noise of a vehicle grinding its way up the muddy lane. An open jeep edged into the yard and two tall, fit-looking soldiers climbed out to stretch and look around. Finding a young Irishman in a white soutane standing in a steamy yard outside a western bungalow in the middle of rice fields probably added to their collection of, 'You'd-never-believe-it' stories of Korea but they quickly recovered from their surprise.

After introductions, I helped them with their baggage into the house and one asked, 'Is it OK to take in some beer?' He indicated a crate of cans in the back of the vehicle. I hadn't seen any alcohol in the house when I arrived so I apologised and told them they were welcome to bring in whatever they had. That was probably another story for them to pass on, 'An Irishman in a house with no beer!'

As we went in, the more talkative soldier looked back at the empty yard and remarked, 'It's very quiet here, isn't it? What do you do in the evening?' Seeing my hesitation he added, 'Do you have some girls up from the Ville?'

In US military language, the 'Ville' is the collection of houses around the camp gate, the place they go for drinks and the company of women. I wondered for a moment was he suggesting that I get girls for them. He saw my confusion and asked, 'What do you do in this place anyhow?'

The question silenced me. Unless he was a Southern Baptist he wouldn't be impressed by my saying I was there to save souls.

If I told him I was there to help set up the Church in Korea, he might point to the deserted compound outside and ask is that what I meant. I could think of no reply that might sound reasonable and still be honest.

The soldiers didn't wait for a response, they brought their bags into the house, tidied up and set off to find the Sisters' house.

When I was alone again, I sat down and tried to work out why I had been caught out so easily.

I had never discussed our motivation with my five classmates who came with me to Korea less than a year previously. It was obvious, or so we thought. 'Saving souls' would be the ready answer but what 'saving' meant was something we never talked about. Already it was losing its literal meaning but no one challenged it openly and in some form or other it would continue to motivate many over the coming years.

How long the old concept of salvation survived was made clear to me some twenty years later when I was visiting a colleague in Chang-ho-wan, outside Seoul. On the way back by bus a young man came up and sat beside me. He was a thin, serious-looking student wanting to engage the foreigner in conversation so he could practice his English.

We started talking slowly in English but soon changed to Korean. I had years of Korean language studies behind me by then, he had only his high school English.

I asked him what he was doing in the town we had just left. He said he was a student at a two-year Christian Theology College. What would he do when he graduated? He would go to China as a missionary.

'China?' I asked, becoming more interested. 'But you can't get a visa to evangelise in China.'

'Oh, I know that,' he replied. 'I would just go in with a visitor's visa and disappear.'

I was both curious and impressed.

'And why would you do that?' I enquired, 'Is it not very dangerous?'

'It would be worth going just to save one soul,' he responded solemnly.

I paused for a moment.

'I can sympathise with you,' I said. 'When I came to Korea, twenty years ago, I was thinking on those lines. However when I came to appreciate Korean traditions and the way people respected each other I said to myself, "Surely not all of their ancestors are doomed. Many of them lived in a way that any Christian could be proud of," and that made me think again.'

It was his turn to be silent. Then he faced me and replied in a troubled voice, 'That's the one thing that bothers me, the one doubt that gives me concern.'

We were entering Seoul by this time. I knew our talking time was running out but was afraid I might have ruined his vocation as a missionary. I told him that when he got back to college he should talk with one of his professors and think more on the issue. We parted in a chastened mood.

Back in Kangjin in 1964, my missionary reasoning was not as rigorous as his but the question put by the American sergeant must have been lurking in the back of my mind, waiting for someone to challenge me with it.

We had arrived in Korea with a sense of identity based on the role we would play in setting up the Church. Even if we were not sure what that meant, we would soon be told what to do and shown how. The men there before us, veterans who had lived through the Korean War, had the answers. We just had to be patient and learn from them.

However, I had a feeling that it might not be so simple. That day in Kangjin, I began to face up to the fact there must be more to our work than just setting up an institution that was beginning to lose credibility back home. If the people in Ireland were beginning to question some of the assumptions of the Church, such as its understanding of salvation, should we be duplicating that situation in Korea?

I looked around the bookshelves of the absent pastor for help. There were just a few dusty novels and the same theological books I had studied as a student. The Vatican Council had opened in Rome two years earlier to review the Church's place in the modern world and new attitudes were emerging but they would take some time to reach Korea.

The only other book was a Bible and a thought struck me. If I were a Buddhist I would be teaching, 'This is what Buddha said,' if I were a Confucian scholar l would be repeating the words of Confucius so, as a follower of Jesus of Nazareth, shouldn't I be reporting what he said? Going back to the Bible for answers was not normal practice for Catholics but lacking other resources it seemed the obvious thing to do.

So, what exactly was the message? Despite four years of scripture studies and theology it was the first time I asked myself that question. I put aside all thoughts of Church doctrines and began to read the gospels to get a sense of what Jesus actually said.

The first gospel was Matthew's and I skipped through the stories of Jesus's birth. When I reached, 'From that time Jesus began to preach,' I felt, 'This must be it.' What he said was, 'Prepare, for the Kingdom of heaven is at hand'. The next three chapters were all about this 'Kingdom of heaven.' He was obviously not talking about heaven and hell, sin and superstition, but about the poor, those who mourn, those who hunger, the meek, peacemakers and the persecuted. It seemed the Kingdom was not a place, heaven, but about people, and about this world.

I was annoyed that I was discovering something this basic so late, yet everyone trained in my generation would have to go through a similar shift in understanding sooner or later. We had been instructed in what to believe but not in how to search for the truth.

It was a more significant moment than I realised and it didn't immediately transform my life. I was a raw newcomer, part of a deferential society, and conscious that I had a lot to learn from the veterans. Yet, the doubts in my mind had been elevated to a conscious level and, as the gurus say, wisdom becomes available once the mind is opened by doubt.

***

That autumn I got my first appointment to a parish and an opportunity to learn from one of the most highly regarded veterans, Tommy Moran. While the thought of working with such an austere figure was slightly intimidating, the location of the parish attracted me. I was going to Jeju Island, my first choice if I had been asked.

If I am in a place for any length of time I want to know who lived there previously, what physical remains hint at how they lived, where the side roads lead. Language limitations and a shortage of written materials meant it took time to get to know Jeju and its people but it was worth the wait.

The island is fifty miles off the south coast of Korea, its most southerly point. Now it is a popular tourist resort known as 'Honeymoon Island' and in 2002, almost forty years later, was host to several matches in the Soccer World Cup. However at that time it was basic. Few Koreans could afford to go there on vacation and it had only one Western-style hotel. The population of 300,000 lived in villages around the coast as the interior of the island was dominated by a dormant volcano, Mount Halla, with rocky and less than fertile slopes. Life was hard and the Jejuites were a sturdy people, making a living from fishing and tilling the stony soil. Only an outsider, with the leisure to admire the sweeping vista from Mount Halla to the sea and the white unspoilt beaches, could imagine its future as a tourist paradise.

I travelled to Jeju on 25 September 1964 on a Korea Air Lines DC3. I noted the date because it was the feast of the Korean Martyrs and while I was in no hurry to be a martyr it seemed an auspicious date for someone getting actively involved in the Korean Church. The flight from Seoul took just over one hour, going by train and ferry would have taken two or three days.

At that time there were five parishes on the island, all staffed by Columbans. Indeed there were no other foreigners on the island except at a small U.S. radar facility in Mosulpo, monitoring air traffic including what was taking off and landing in Mao Zedong's Shanghai, over the western horizon.

Catholics in the city numbered about three thousand. Their modest church had been built by French missionaries eighty years previously. It was one of the few red-brick structures on the island and had a bell tower that was visible from most parts of town. Beside it was a girls' school run by Korean St Paul de Chartres Sisters.

The pastor, Tommy Moran, was a Roscommon man almost twenty years older than me and a legend in the diocese for his zeal and thoroughness. He saw himself as my mentor and patiently set about showing me how things should be done and why. Often our main meal would drag on an extra hour or two as he tried to answer my cautiously posed questions until he thought I got it straight. I never asked him his motivation for being there, he would have been shocked to hear that I did not know the answer already.

One day at lunch he told me he had just spent an hour talking with a young man who was planning to marry a non-Catholic lady. My pastor advised him to put off the wedding for six months or a year as the girl in question was an orphan.

He explained, 'Since she is an orphan, she never really experienced love when she was young and will make great demands on whoever she marries. However, if she comes to the church first and learns about God's love for her, then she will be in a better position to love her husband and receive his love.'

I was amazed at Tommy's confidence and his forthright advice. Non-directive counselling was not yet in fashion. Yet his sincerity and determination to help were so strong people could not but be impressed. He had served in some of the biggest parishes in Kwangju diocese, and would continue to do so for many more years, and was revered everywhere as a saint.

My language skills were still at a basic level so I was not expected to preach but I was put in charge of the students' Legion of Mary groups and had to give them a weekly pep talk, carefully written out and corrected beforehand. My pastor was a big promoter of the Legion, an organisation to get Catholics active in their parish, and already it was becoming the most popular and effective lay group in the Korean Church.

Its members were given a weekly duty to perform and reported on it at the next meeting. Usually the task was to go out in pairs to visit those who were not coming regularly to the church. My role was to accompany the Junior Legionaries on their visits. Thanks to them I would get out of the confines of the parish compound and into the life of the city itself. I could begin to see how people managed to live in an environment completely different from anything I had known.

From then on, once or twice a week, with two student companions I travelled the lanes of JeJu city in search of absentee young Catholics. Being students themselves, the Legionaries were good guides but, unlike later years, I was seldom invited into homes. I was merely the assistant priest who wanted to talk to students and had not much Korean but the people also felt somewhat ashamed of their houses and the lack of means to show hospitality.

It did not take me long to get a sense of the religious environment. Walking along the narrow winding lanes, bordered by high walls of grey volcanic rocks, I passed local spirit shrines and was regularly deafened by the loud drumming and singing of *kuts*, the shamanist séances. Jeju had its own forms of shamanism which enjoyed widespread patronage. Obviously this was part of the 'superstition' I had been warned about but there was no encouragement or means to find out what was going on behind those stone walls.

The students were proud of their island home and explained that Jeju is famous for three things: its women, wind and stones.

The women were the backbone of the economy, many working as *hae-nye* or sea divers. They were trained from an early age to stay underwater for long spells and harvested the seabed for shellfish and other edibles. Back on the surface they made a loud cooing sound that echoed around the Island. No one could tell me whether it was to clear their lungs or let others know where they were.

Later the tourist board was to picture the *hae-nye* as lissome young ladies in skimpy dress but those I knew were in their thirties or forties and wore long white swimming clothes.

Usually their husbands were at home tending their small plot of land so the men had the reputation of being lazy and families as being matriarchal. As often happens in church communities, the women did most of the work there too. However, few of the students would volunteer the information that their mothers were *hae-nye*. Already the profession was looked down on as old-fashioned and a sign of poverty.

The strong winds that swept across Jeju were typical of most exposed islands and the thatched roofs of the houses were tightly tied down with straw ropes. The coldest blasts came during the first few months of the year but they affected my expeditions around the city only when a storm sent waves crashing across the narrow causeways on the seafront. Most of the year blue, sunny skies were common and the clear air was ideal for photography.

Islands are also likely to be rocky and because of its volcanic origins Jeju is boulder-strewn from Halla's bald head to the petrified ridges of lava reaching out into the sea and dubbed with poetic names like 'Dragonhead Rock.' Stones gathered from the fields are stacked up in high walls which help protect the soil from been blown away by the winds. The grey rock is also the principal building material, there were few concrete or brick buildings.

I soon discovered that Jejuites have a strong sense of self-identity with their own language, traditions and origin myths. The three founding families were the Kos, Yangs and Bues and those names still predominated. I was shown the 'Three Holy Openings' from which those ancestors emerged out of the earth.

However, once you are accepted as a 'Jejuite,' a special bond is formed and the Jeju Catholics had a strong affection for their priests, especially those who had stayed with them during the difficult years. They expected, and hoped, that the priests whom they got to know well would never leave and be buried there. A number are.

Despite the distractions of *hae-nye*, wind, rocks and the natural beauty of the island, I was supposed to be concentrating on the errant students. When we found them they usually turned out to be shy, polite boys and girls dressed, even at home, in their Japanese-style uniforms. The boys wore back jackets, with brass buttons up to the neck, and flat-peaked caps, reminding me of railway porters. The girls' jackets were topped by sailor-uniform bibs. Some were not coming to church because their parents insisted that they study 15 hours a day, including weekends. Such study was normal but most Catholic families allowed their children a few hours off on Sundays. It was my job to persuade the parents of the non-attenders that going to Sunday Mass would have a beneficial effect, even on their studies.

Still, when it came to cultural lessons I had no school. I had to learn the hard way, from my mistakes.

One day I was invited to go to a cemetery on the side of Mt Halla, to the grave of a young boy who had been leader of the altar servers club. He died the previous year. It was a hot October morning and the tomb was halfway up the mountain, over two hours walk. When we finally got there we gathered in a circle with the family to offer incense and recite prayers. By the time the memorial service was over it was noon and I was both thirsty and hungry. The daughter of the family, Angela, a lovely twenty-year old girl and a Legion leader, offered me a bowl of water with both hands.

'This is just what I need,' I thought and greedily started drinking. I had almost emptied it when I became aware of her astonished gaze and realised I had done something wrong. The water was for washing my hands and not for drinking. We were both embarrassed at my loss of 'face.'

As members of a Confucian society, Koreans show great respect for elders and teachers. Though I was only twenty-six, I rated as both elder and teacher so Angela had offered me the bowl with both hands. As a 'superior person' I should at least have known what to do with it but I had shown complete ignorance. Not that anyone said anything, their instinctive effort to cover up any reaction was all that alerted me to my error.

I gradually learned that in any formal situation there is only one 'right way' of behaviour when it came to greeting, refusing, eating and celebrating. This strict code of civility is based not only on showing respect for people but was also extending to nature and beyond. It was vaguely familiar and attractive. Where did it came from? Was it due to one of their religions? Few seemed interested in my questions, whatever about being able to answer them.

Despite my language and cultural limitations l tried to be useful. One of my duties was to supervise catechism classes for primary school children. Five days a week, the children came to the church after school where the Sisters and some lay teachers taught them for an hour. I could not contribute to the teaching, which was mainly recitation of the catechism, but I could ensure that attendance stayed high.

Here my Western enterprise surfaced. I awarded each student a star sticker for every day they attended and when they got thirty or more I gave them a holy picture or other religious article as a reward. To build up the supply of prizes l wrote an article about my project for our Columban monthly magazines in Ireland, the US and Australia and soon, despite the distances involved, I was receiving a regular supply of pictures, rosaries and small statues from all over the world, especially Australia.

The local post office noted this rise in imports and tried to tax me on each parcel. At the beginning I was happy to pay a small sum but gradually the demand increased. In the end I sent them an ultimatum that if they did not go back to the original sum l would leave the parcels on their hands. As they were not likely to find much of a market for second-hand Christian religious articles, they relented and we reached an agreement. I was learning how to cope with local bureaucracies though I also felt a little guilty about flooding the island with foreign religious items.

Gradually I began to see what the Church meant to the people of Jeju.

The Catholic Church had not always been popular on the island which was very traditional and suspicious of outsiders, even fellow Koreans from the mainland. French missionaries went there in 1886 under the terms of a Franco-Korean treaty which gave special privileges to the missionaries and their followers. This led to complaints that Catholic converts were misusing their affiliation and had unfair tax advantages. In 1901 villagers on the eastern side of the island got together in protest and attacked Jeju City where most of the Catholics lived. A massacre followed in which 300 local Catholics were killed.

However the French left one good memory behind them. They introduced mandarin oranges to the western side of the island which became valuable income-earners known as 'university trees.' It was said that with one or two of them you could send a child on to third-level education.

When the Columbans first arrived in 1934, during the Japanese colonial period, there were still bad feelings towards Catholics among people in the eastern villages. However when two of the missionaries were imprisoned for not showing proper respect for the detested Japanese Emperor, attitudes began to change. One of the priests, Pat Dawson, spent seven years in jail doing hard labour for his lack of Imperial respect and when, after the war, the missionaries were active in helping the people recover their livelihood, their stock rose even further.

When I arrived I could see that much of the respect in which the Church was held, by both Catholics and non-Catholics, was due to those earlier priests, people like Beatrice Choi and Fr PJ McGlinchey.

Beatrice was the head of Jeju Provincial Education Department. A medical doctor by profession, she had been actively involved in the resistance movement during the Japanese occupation and was considered a national heroine. Though now a high public official, she lived in an unassuming straw-roofed traditional Jeju house with her mother. When I called there once a month to visit her mother, she would be standing outside waiting with a lighted candle.

Small in height and slightly rotund, she always dressed in subdued Korean fashion, impressing by her simplicity and quiet authority. She must have had great influence in parish affairs but she never seemed to interfere. Around the town just a mention of her name opened doors and made projects possible.

Another icon of the Jeju Church, still alive and on the island, is Fr PJ McGlinchey from Donegal who first went there in 1953 and has never left except on vacation.

On the barren slopes of Halla he built a pig farm along cooperative lines, developed grass that could survive on the volcanic slopes and imported sheep to provide the materials for a local 'Irish Tweed' factory. Later he added a retreat house and youth centre, as well as setting up a stud farm (with Irish thoroughbreds) for the local racing industry. He was awarded a number of national and international prizes and so impressed President Park Chug-hee in the late 1960s that he ordered the road from the coast to the farm be tarred and invited him to the Presidential Palace in Seoul to lecture his ministers on what could be done for the country.

Due to the goodwill created by prominent Catholics like Beatrice, the wartime Columbans and PJ, the five parishes on Jeju were buzzing in 1964. The number of adults entering the Church was small but steady and there were enough activities to keep the men there busy.

However life was not all work and on Mondays the eight Columbans on the island got together, usually in Moselpo where they could go to a movie at the army camp attached to the radar station. In the afternoon we would head for the mountainside to chase pheasants. They were so plentiful, and other meat so scarce, that we had pheasant at every meal. Helena, our cook in Jeju city, had a dozen different ways of preparing it but an occasional dish of fish was appreciated.

Often in the autumn around 4.00 pm I would drag myself from my language studies and drive out in the parish jeep, using the excuse of hunting to immerse myself in the countryside. I would walk for miles with Tom, an enthusiastic but untrained pointer, across the sunny, open mountainside, climbing over stone walls. On one side was Mt Halla and on the other the seashore below. Sometimes a pheasant would even jump up with a screech to disturb the quiet and if I missed I had no regrets. One less bird to eat. If I hit one, Tom would likely bury it in a hole before I got to it.

My social life was limited outside the Columban circle. The people I met most often in the parish were the volunteers who ran the Sunday school or the Junior Legion and even if they did not have jobs and families to look after they had no money to entertain me and there were few places in the town suitable for relaxing.

One day Tommy brought two young ladies into my office. They were mainlanders who lectured at Jeju University, a greyish-black structure built with rough Jeju rock out near the airport. In his usual helpful way Tommy suggested that I practice my Korean with them while they practiced their English on me. The arrangement suited both parties and lasted for a few months. Though my Korean was not great, nor their English, chatting with two intelligent young ladies in both languages helped pass the day when the Jeju wind was howling outside.

They were from the northern province of Kangwon-do and found themselves treated as foreigners by the locals. Neither of them was Christian but they were interested in the church and what it stood for.

One day we were discussing the difference between the Christian God and the Korean heavenly spirit, *Ha-nu-nim*, when I mentioned that a characteristic of Jesus was his emphasis on God's love (*sarang*) for humans.

'Love?' they exclaimed, 'Do you use the word "love," *sarang*, for God?' There were a number of words for 'love' in Korean, two of them based on Chinese characters and indicating 'affection' or 'care.' '*Sarang*' was a more popular vernacular Korean word that had recently become common in romantic novels and pop songs.

'Yes,' I said, '*Sarang* is the word we use.'

I could see the concept intrigued them but hoped that neither Tommy nor the office man were passing the door and heard us talking about *sarang*.

From Tommy I learnt how the Catholic Church operated in Korea. It had a hierarchical and authoritarian style that suited the people's Confucian outlook and they had no complaint. It was the sort of Church that Tommy was brought up in also and he did not see any reason for it to change. I was not so happy with its emphasis on uniformity in Church practices all around the world and Tommy never really succeeded in converting me.

On Sundays I would say Mass in one of the two outstations where my language limitations would do little damage. The catechist organised everything and I had little personal contact with the people living on subsistence level in those seaside, high-walled villages. Life was basic but the people came faithfully, prayed and hurried home. Before they left they would often ask, 'Can I have a dispensation to work today?' Prohibition against working on the Lord's Day was still in force but exceptions easily given.

On the one-or-two-hour trips to those villages we passed the clean white and deserted beach at Hamdek. In summer, coming back I would get Andy, the driver, to stop there. He would have a smoke while I dashed into the warm water and enjoyed a brief swim. Passing fishermen, and probably Andy himself, were bemused by the foreigner out there by himself. For the hardworking Jeju people, relaxing time was when you lay down and slept, not swam in the sea.

I was closer to the people in Jeju city than those in the outstations but they were of little help when I looked for information on the local history and culture.

'That's the way it always was,' they would answer though perhaps they realised any more complicated explanation would be beyond my language capability. Yet they were unfailingly kind and patient. The fact that I was a priest in their church was a help but their graciousness went beyond that, overlooking the fact that I was a foreigner, young and not able to do much to help them.

When I went to Jeju, or Korea for that matter, the idea of learning something from the people was not considered a priority. I was more curious than expectant, intrigued by the way the people acted, built houses, ate and even thought differently. However I was too convinced of the superiority of my Western ways and religious beliefs to suppose I could become a better person by listening to them. It was in Jeju that my attitude began to change. I could see something attractive in the way the people believed and behaved despite their poverty but all this was still too vague and 'foreign' to make any serious impact on my reasoning. However, the seed had been planted.

For many years afterwards I would go back to Jeju for my summer vacation. The people I had known would greet me as if I had never left, letting my Columban friends from the mainland know I was one of theirs. I had lived with them, learnt a few words of their dialect and knew some of their ways. I would walk the familiar paths between the high stone walls, climb Halla Mountain and taste the fresh water springs that appeared in the sand when the tide went out in Hamdek. It was like returning to one's roots.

Recently Jeju has attracted international headlines because the United States is building a major naval base there. Anti-war activists, anti-American radicals and Christian groups object strongly as they fear it is the start of another Cold War in an area where the ownership of islands and oil rights are disputed by China and is neighbours. However, when I left there life was much simpler and the most urgent question on my mind was how I would cope with life back on the mainland with its more sophisticated cities and demands. If I was to make any contribution I would need to be fluent in the language and more at home in local customs and ways of thinking. We had been told that 'East is East and West is West and never the twain shall meet,' but Jeju had reassured me that the differences were not as deep as claimed and we had far more in common than anyone suspected.

Chapter 2
Minor Diplomat

The autumn after leaving Jeju I re-joined my classmates in Seoul for another six months at language school, this time at Yon-sae University. We did not realise at the time how much our language studies would change our way of thinking.

As Westerners, we were confident that we could assist the East by encouraging individualism, the sense of personal autonomy, freedom and being master of one's own destiny. We had been told Orientals were too bound down by family ties and fatalism to rise to the challenge of creating anything new or progressive. Christianity and individualism also seemed closely related. If you believed in a personal call to be a Christian and that God's Spirit demanded an individual response, you should not be held back by the ties of relationships or fatalism.

That we had such an attitude was exposed during our language studies. Korean de-emphasised 'me.' Instead of 'I' or 'my' it is 'we' and 'our.' You don't say, 'I'm leaving,' but simply, 'Going, now.' It is not, 'my country or family' but 'our country,' or as they would say, 'Our Korea' or 'Our China.' Similarly, you do not draw attention to yourself by directly expressing your desires or feelings. Rather you pointed out the quality of the object in question by saying, 'It is very tasty.' Immediately your host would know that you liked it and insist you take more of it. If you said to a girl, 'You are very beautiful,' it could be the equivalent of, 'I like you.'

Asians, especially East Asians, are very conscious of age, rank and relationships. The first question a Korean, or Chinese, will ask you is, 'When were you born?' (The second question a Chinese will ask is, 'How much do you earn?') They need to know whether you are older or younger than them so they can address you properly. If you are older or have a higher social rank they must use 'high' language. That usually means formal words, like 'dine' instead of 'eat', or 'repose' rather than 'sleep,' but various grades of verb endings are also added to show proper respect.

Later, when I was in Shillim Dong and taking part in pro-democracy demonstrations, we would gather in a wine house afterwards to recover from our encounter with the riot police and review the event. On one such occasion a group of our fellow-demonstrators at the next table had a noisy disagreement. Two of them were standing up, hurling insults at each other and ready to exchange blows. I asked one of my companions what had happened.

'Oh,' he replied, 'They were talking and one of them did not address his senior with proper respect.'

I was impressed that young people out risking their lives, or bones, for democracy a short time previously would, minutes later, be upset about not showing the proper deference due to differences in age. However, they were going through a transformation that also faced us as we studied the language, though in reverse. We were moving from a culture which encouraged us to assert what 'I' felt and wanted, to one that constantly reminded us that 'we' are part of society with roles to play as younger brother, parent, senior student or junior manager. The young Koreans were heading in the opposite cultural direction.

Where the Korean language survives, respect for others will not be ignored. There are at least three levels of speech: 'high' for a person older or of more honourable rank, 'low' for a younger person and a 'middle' for informal occasions. We felt uncomfortable using the 'low form' to young people. It did not seem right to be speaking 'down' even to children but if we used a higher level they would just laugh at our mistake.

This Oriental show of humility, of de-emphasising oneself, is often misunderstood by Westerners who may view it as insincere and backward. We didn't understand it fully at the time but we knew that if we wanted to speak Korean properly we just had to talk that way. Gradually our attitude changed and even today I find myself using 'we' more than 'I'. 'Who is this "we" you are talking about?' my friends ask.

I had little idea at the time that I was encountering the tip of an iceberg--a world view that had once been common to most of

humanity but had been overlaid in the West by an individualistic
approach. Importance was given to the role one is expected
to play in society. Rather than been known and addressed as
'Jack' or 'Jill,' you are hailed as 'Teacher,' 'Older Sister,' 'Section
Chief,' 'Uncle' (because of age, rather than family relationship)
or 'Reverend Father.' It was the Chinese who had developed this
sense of duty and responsibility to a high degree.

Being forced to change my approach to individuality was
only a start; later I also had to accept that my tendency to regard
Korean religions and 'fatalism' as superstitious and backward
deserved similar readjustment.

However there were few opportunities in Seoul at that time
to delve deeper into the culture, introductory classes and books
did not exist. Fortunately, that would shortly change.

Our first opportunity to take Korea seriously was offered
by Paul S Crane, the son of Presbyterian missionaries. Born in
1919, he spent his childhood in Korea and spoke the language
fluently. Later he was to be the official interpreter for US
Presidents visiting Korea. As a doctor-missionary he helped
found the Presbyterian Hospital in Chonju and Han Nam
University in Taejon. In the early 1960s he began to write for *The
Korea Times* on his observations of Korean life and published
a popular book, *Korean Patterns*. It was the first systematic
reflection on the life and traditions of the people by a foreigner
and became a textbook for newcomers wanting to learn more.

What he did was to apply the findings of anthropology to
culture and religion. One method was to search for 'patterns of
culture,' habits and practices that could be seen as distinguishing
one culture from another. Paul Crane began to list the unique
traits and patterns he found in Korean life.

I read his book avidly. His descriptions of how Korean people
can be expected to behave in different circumstances seemed
accurate and led me to ask, 'Why?' I wanted to know the
reason people acted that way. Was it Confucianism, Buddhism,
Taoism, Shamanism or something uniquely Korean? We had
never studied any of those 'isms' during our training but now
we had fewer excuses.

***

After two three-month semesters at the language school, I was appointed to Kwangju, the capital of Cholla province and once more to the care of Tommy Moran who had moved to the cathedral there after leaving Jeju. Perhaps fortunately for both of us we were reunited for only a short time.

Tommy was as dedicated and serious as ever but my questions were becoming more taxing and the after-dinner conversations were getting longer. Some of the breakthrough following Vatican II was finding its way to Korea but Tommy saw little need for change. He was busy at that time doing a new translation of the Legion Handbook and the Legion continued to prove itself an effective way of involving people in the parish. Its formality, weekly duties and militaristic line-of-command structure suited the Korean mentality. However my language ability was improving and I wanted to do more than monitor the Junior Legion and children's classes.

Kwangju was a regional capital as far back as 57 BC but little evidence remained of any past glory or ancient history. The destruction of the recent war was reflected in its narrow dusty streets, lined with unimpressive single-storey shops. However the old cathedral at Bukdong, near the centre and not far from the railway station, had survived. Every morning about 2.00 am, the steam engines would start shunting with whistles and shrieks that were hard to ignore. The road between the church and the station was a 'Red Light' area and every time I walked up it a crowd of young and older women would come running to greet me but turn away when they recognised who I was. 'It's only the priest,' they would shout, some giving me a friendly wave and others inviting me in despite my collar.

One day I was asked to visit an invalid near the station. We went down the 'Red Light' street but instead of turning towards the station square we veered to the right and into the mouth of what looked like a tunnel. Following the catechist, I went down the ramp and found myself in a cavern divided by planks into two floors of living spaces with no more than a combined height of twelve feet. To get to the upper dwellings we climbed a short ladder and crept into a narrow room that was used for cooking, dining, work and sleep. The sick lady lay the on the floor with her family gathered around her.

I was used to the unexpected but it took me a while to absorb what I had seen. This was life at the basic level. People lived there, went out to work or school each day, returned, ate and slept there. Yet no one complained or looked for sympathy. Things would get better, and they did, and life would go on.

Such 'primary shelters' were usually situated near railway stations, convenient for families migrating to the cities. Nearly twenty years later I would see a similar sight near Yong-dong-po station in Seoul and could only marvel at how little had changed for some families. Back in Kwangju we were, or at least Tommy was, aware of their situation but with everyone struggling to make a living little special attention was given to those 'upper bunk, lower bunk' families. They came to the church on equal terms with everyone else and disappeared afterwards.

I didn't have time to get to know Kwangju well. I was there only a few months when Tommy told me one morning that the bishop wanted to see me. Wondering if I had done something wrong, I went off on my newly acquired motor cycle to his house outside the city.

The bishop was an affable American, Harold Henry, and he lost no time in telling me that he was sending me to Seoul to work as secretary in the Vatican Embassy or Nunciature. I had only met him on a few social occasions but he assured me he was confident l would have no trouble meeting any demands put on me. In fact I think my main qualification was that I could type.

My acquaintance with Kwangju was short so I had no regret in loading my luggage back on the train and returning to Seoul. Fifteen years later I was to return to a transformed Kwangju, more modern but in the centre of a people's uprising.

**

A Nunciature is a Papal Embassy but I had a hard time explaining that to Korean officials. If it was an embassy in Korean, a *tae-sa-gwan*, why was it not an embassy in English instead of calling it a 'Nunciature'? And what was the *Kyo-hwang-chong* (the Korean translation for Vatican) anyhow? It did not sound like a country. The Korean title translated literally as, 'Church Leader Government' so you could hardly blame them.

The office/residence of the Nunciature is in a quiet zone near the Presidential Blue House and at that time had a staff of two with full diplomatic status, the Nuncio and a Secretary. I was an attaché with a diplomatic identity card and a tiny Fiat 500 sporting diplomatic plates. When one of the two permanent men was away I lived in the Nunciature, otherwise I commuted Monday to Friday from the Columban central house three miles away.

My main duties were to mark and clip out newspaper articles that might be of interest to the Vatican, attend to some correspondence, translate for local visitors and do odd jobs that the Italian Nuncio and his Lithuanian-English Secretary could not or did not want to handle. They had no Korean.

A lot of the diplomatic correspondence concerned the movement of personnel: 'The Embassy of X wishes to inform the Holy See that Mr Y will serve in Korea as third trade secretary. The Embassy of X takes this opportunity to assure the Holy See of its deep respect and desire to continue friendly ties.'

Sometimes the Secretary would look over my shoulder when I was reading a note from the American Embassy and comment on the arrival of a new Third Cultural Secretary, 'Oh, a new man for the CIA, I see.'

It was my duty to reply, 'The Holy See wishes to acknowledge receipt of your kind greetings on Z date and the announcement of Mr Y's appointment. The Holy See takes this opportunity to assure the Embassy of X of the high regard of the Holy See.' The formula was always the same and it could be quite boring.

However, early on the Secretary told me a story as a warning. One of my predecessors had got a note informing the Nunciature that the Japanese Government had built a lighthouse on Takeshima Island in the Eastern Sea which, they stated, would be of great assistance to shipping. He replied as usual that the Holy See had gratefully received this news, congratulated the Japanese government on its lighthouse and took the opportunity to wish Japan well.

Takeshima also has a Korean name, Tok-do, and is stoutly claimed by the Korean nation. Soon the Korean Department of Foreign Affairs was asking the Vatican whether the letter indicated that the Holy See recognised Japan's claim to Tok-do? Apologies had to be made all around and whoever wrote the letter was told off. Today Korea and Japan are still arguing over Takeshima/Tok-do.

The range of cuttings I was expected to take from Korean newspapers to send to Rome made me aware of how widespread Vatican interests were and why it is considered one of the top listening posts in the world. The analysts back in Rome were interested not only in religious and political developments but in economics, population, culture and governance. Everything but sport.

In October the Nunciature was asked to send its military attaché to attend a memorial service to be held in the southern city of Pusan for those killed in the Korean War. I was sent to represent the Swiss Guard, or so the Secretary said. The American Air Force would fly us from its base on Yoi-do on the Han River. I was there in plenty of time but take-off was delayed by the late arrival of an archetypal British Brigadier, red-faced and moustachioed, dressed in black with red trimmings, and trailing a long sword. A Korean army officer beside me smiled and said it reminded him of the Japanese.

When we were on the bus going from Pusan airport to the cemetery, the Brigadier sat near me and introduced himself. His name was Brainridge and in an upper-class British accent he asked, 'What part of Ireland do you come from, Father?'

'Dublin,' I replied.

'I come from Ballyragget myself,' he responded.

Presuming that it could not be part of England, I asked him what part of Northern Ireland that might be. 'Eleven miles from Kilkenny,' he said.

I was to meet him again on a number of tenser occasions: two Irishmen in Korea, one representing Great Britain and the other the Swiss Guard.

On the 16 January 1968, thirty-one members of an elite North Korean commando force left their base in the North and crossed over the mountainous area through the American army division guarding the border into the south. They belonged to the officer-rank Unit 124 and had trained for long marches over rough terrain. Their mission was to kill the South Korean president, Park Chung-hee, who lived in the Blue House, just four hundred yards from the Nunciature.

On the 19th they camped in the hills outside Seoul. Four wood-cutting brothers named Wu stumbled on them and were taken prisoner. Instead of killing or tying them up, the North Koreans confided that they had come to liberate the South which was colonised by the Americans and their camp-followers. The brothers gave the impression they were grateful to the North Koreans for this but on being released they ran to the nearest police station and reported the incident. Immediately the alarm was sounded.

Two days later, on Saturday the 21st, I was showing some of my confreres from the country around Seoul in my little Fiat. On the way back there were checkpoints set up on the bridges over the Han River. We were not stopped because of my diplomatic plates but obviously something serious was happening. Security had been comparatively slack up till then and nothing unusual was reported on the news that night.

The North Koreans had split up into two and three-man-cells and reunited on Saturday night at a temple outside Seoul. There they changed into South Korean uniforms, wearing the correct badges for the Southern 26th Infantry Division. By 10.00 pm on Sunday they had marched to within a half mile of the Blue House when they were stopped at a checkpoint. The Nunciature was halfway between them and their target and the unsuspecting Secretary was there on his own as the Nuncio had just left and not yet been replaced.

The officer in charge of the checkpoint was Choi Gyu-shik, the police commander of Chong-no central district. I had met him the previous September when he came to make a courtesy call at the Nunciature. He was an energetic young man in his thirties, married with two children, and had been baptised in the Catholic Church the previous August 15 taking the name Peter. He was delighted that the Nunciature was in his district and offered to be of any service he could. He told me he was studying business administration at the nearby Buddhist University and I could see that he would rise quickly on the promotion ladder.

The suicide squad stopped short of the checkpoint and shouted that they were a patrol out on a counter-infiltration exercise. Commander Choi went forward to inspect them and quickly realised who they really were. He tried to pull his gun out of its holster but was shot immediately. His men back at the checkpoint began firing at the North Koreans who split up and fled into the surrounding hills.

I returned to the Nunciature on Monday morning knowing nothing of what had happened. The media has not yet reported anything and phones were blocked. As I came near the residence I could see groups of armed police and soldiers coming out of houses they had searched. No one tried to stop me. The Secretary was waiting impatiently. He knew no Korean and had heard guns going off all around him during the night but couldn't find out what was happening. From the security guard at the gate I got an early version of the story and relayed it to the Secretary who was not reassured to hear there were still over twenty North Koreans in the area killing people.

In the ensuing manhunt, one North Korean, Kim Shin-Jo, was captured, one was never found and 29 were killed. In all 25 South Koreans were killed and 60 wounded during the incident.

Conspiracy theories were already common in Korea and there were rumours that the soldiers were really South Koreans who had mutinied. To counteract this, the American and Korean CIAs held a briefing and display of captured weapons to which we 'Military Attachés' were invited.

The display of weapons proved nothing, they could have come from anywhere, but the description of how the North Koreans had trained for the attack across frozen terrain and details of the route they followed were convincing. The official version was never seriously doubted and today there is a monument to Commander Choi Gyu-shik on the road where the checkpoint stood near the Nunciature.

A few days after the commando attack another event occurred which brought the Cold War temperature in Korea down further.

On 23 January, a US intelligence-gathering ship, the USS *Pueblo*, was captured by the North Korean navy. The Americans claimed it was in international waters; the North Koreans claimed it was in theirs. Soon news got out that the boat had been brought to Wonsan in North Korea and the eighty-three crew members were in a prison camp.

It was a delicate time with the Tet Offensive in Vietnam and the South Koreans considering retaliation against the North for the attempt to assassinate their President. B-51s with nuclear bombs flew up from Guam, turned at the border and went back. Negotiations continued all year and in December the Americans were released after an apology was made. Today the *Pueblo* is a showpiece in the capital of North Korea, used to introduce children and tourists to the evils of the United States and the bravery of North Korean soldiers.

From our arrival in Korea we had been aware that the Korean War was not over officially; there was only a truce with on-going, or never-ending, talks in Panmunjom.

With over half a million soldiers on each side, 'Freedom's Frontier' or the De-Militarised Zone (DMZ), was the most heavily guarded border in the world. One of the two Columban dioceses stretched along the boundary so we were always conscious of, though almost immune to, the constant threat. The US Army media regularly issued warnings to those outside the camps to 'park their jeep on the top of a hill and have it pointing south'.

Our men seemed to give the danger little thought, accepting it as part of life in Korea. One, living in the border parish of Chorwan, invited me up to view the DMZ. I went in my little Fiat and was introduced to a young man in civvies who attended the church, he was a member of the Korean CIA.

When we arrived at the border checkpoint, my colleague and his friend got into a jeep and led the way along rough tracks through open fields. I followed on my own in the Fiat hoping it would not break down and leave me exposed under the North Korean observation posts and guns. We finally got to the forward trenches were we were greeted with some surprise; they had never seen foreigners that close to the front line before, not to say a tiny Fiat 500. They allowed us to use their periscopes to look across the border at the 'peace villages' neatly built for propaganda purposes. Loud diatribes denouncing the South were being boomed across so we could hear little of what the soldiers had to say about life on the DMZ. Our guide was much quieter on our return and I felt he had been told off for bringing foreigners into the security area.

Back in Seoul, only 30 miles away and within range of North Korean artillery, life was going on as usual. People were used to the constant threat and ignored it. Even today, when another North Korean outburst threatens world peace, the people who show least concern are those in South Korea. 'The North Koreans cannot afford to go to war,' they say. 'Our country is so small they would blow themselves up along with us.'

Five Columbans had been killed in the first days of the Korean Conflict and the older men among us had lived through the war. Yet the only time I heard the border situation discussed with anxiety was when I worked in the Nunciature, meeting with diplomats and military personnel in the country on short-term postings. They were hoping to get out before war started again but we became less and less excited as one incident followed another and nothing serious happened.

While in the Nunciature I also helped out in Don Am parish, just beside the Columban central house. The church, a cut-stone structure in Western style, had been completed in 1955 with money from St Patricks Cathedral parish in New York. About 3,000 Catholics lived in the area.

There were two other Columbans in the parish, Maurice O'Connor, a New Zealander, and Noel Ryan, a Cork man who had been a year behind me in college. We were of the same generation and spent hours after supper discussing the area and the people there. North Korea was rarely mentioned, we were more concerned with what the recently concluded Vatican Council might have to offer. Again I was in charge of a Legion, this time a closely-knit group of university students who dropped in most afternoons on their way home to regale us with the latest student witticisms and gossip.

Otherwise there were few differences from the parish system in Jeju or Kwangju. The people in the lower part of the parish were comparatively well off while those on the hillsides were refugees in temporary shacks. Residents from the squatter area came and went on equal terms with everyone else but there was no attempt to get the parish involved in their concerns. The separation between Church and society was clear, partly because most Churches ran their own welfare system but also the foreigners were reluctant to make contacts outside Church circles for language and cultural reasons.

One of the attractions of missionary life at that time was the freedom we had from interference by bishops and the Vatican but we were slow to make full use of the opportunity. This did not bother the Catholics much but it should have concerned us. They were good Confucians, happy with the Church as it was and supporting it generously. There was even a steady trickle of newcomers looking to join.

As a part-timer in the parish I was not in a position to experiment with ways of bridging the gap between Korean culture and that of the Catholic Church but I was concerned that we might be doing in Korea exactly what we would have being doing in Ireland, the United States or Australia. Funerals were an example.

Back in the early 1600s, the Italian Jesuit Matteo Ricci and his companions in China had achieved progress in making Christianity acceptable by respecting traditional practices to honour ancestors. Their sensitivity led to a growing network of supportive friends around the county and finally an invitation from the Emperor in Beijing, an unheard of honour. When word of these initiatives got back to Europe, learned men accused the Jesuits of dabbling in superstition and tolerating Chinese culture to the detriment of the Gospel. Eventually the Vatican stepped in and banned not just Ricci's approach but even discussions on the topic. The 'Chinese Rites' ban put an end to the Church's growth in China and was implemented in Korea when the French missionaries went there in 1836, leading to further persecution.

The prohibition ended in 1933 and finally in 1940 the Korean bishops agreed to permit some of the traditional burial practices such as offering food and wine before a picture of the ancestor or a tablet with his or her name on it. The people have a deep bond with their ancestors and sharing food with them expressed those feelings.

It was part of my Nunciature responsibilities to read the Church newspaper and monthly *City and Country Magazine*. In one issue of the weekly paper I came across a series of articles by Fr Lee Chu-Chang, a professor in Seoul seminary, on the Rites.

He summarised the background and explained how the bishops (still half of them Westerners at that time) had finally got around to issuing cautious directives on which elements of the funeral customs could be used and what had to be rejected

I thought this would be useful information for our Catholics and got a local printer to bring it out in a thirty-five page booklet entitled, *A Short Account of the Sacrifice Problem*. Maybe my effort had not much impact on the people of Don Am Dong who had more urgent concerns but I felt that at least I was making a gesture honouring Korean traditions.

At that time there were two daily English language newspapers in Korea, *The Korea Times* which was preferred by foreigners and *The Korean Herald*, which was seen as a government propaganda sheet.

The *Times* was also quite conservative but it had a two-column section called 'The Thoughts of the Times' for which both locals and foreigners were invited to contribute.

While I was in the Nunciature one of our priests, an American based on the east coast, began writing rather controversial articles for 'The Thoughts.' They attracted considerable attention among our men not only because of the contents but for the fact that a Columban was actually writing for the public press!

It went against tradition, and even canon law, for clerics to write without the bishop's permission but times were changing and this man wrote freely without consulting Church authorities.

Many of the 'Thoughts' columns were on aspects of the local culture and written by men like Paul Crane, so one morning at breakfast I plucked up courage and mentioned casually to our Director, 'These articles in the *Times* are interesting, I'm thinking of writing one myself.'

The Director nearly choked on his coffee. 'Why would you do that?' he asked.

He was a nice man and I did not want to offend so I wondered what I could say that might make sense to him.

'I hear they make some sort of financial payment,' I replied lamely, knowing it was only minimal.

'What,' he gasped, 'Do you need money? If you do, l will give it to you.'

The State was just as sensitive about what foreigners were writing.

An American Fulbright scholar made the mistake of publishing an article in the *Korea Times* in which he suggested, jokingly, that to streamline the education system and help the economy, girls coming out of school be divided into two groups: those who had a strong physique should be sent to work in factories and those who were weaker but pretty should go into the hospitality industry and take care of the needs of Japanese tourists. He called it, 'A Modest Proposal,' in the spirit of Jonathan Swift but the government did not see the humour and expelled him from the country.

I was to write over 100 articles on aspects of Korean culture for the 'Thoughts' column in the 70s and 80s but restrained myself during my first tour, conscious of my position in the Nunciature.

As my first six year term in Korea drew to an end, I began to consider what l would like to do on my return from vacation.

I had enjoyed the different experiences that Jeju, Kwangju, the Nunciature and Don Am Dong offered and was beginning to get an idea of how the people reacted to situations in their own distinctive way. But I was aware of the limitations in my understanding of their thinking and behaviour, what they really believed and why certain practices were important to them. If I was to continue to work in Korea, which was what I wanted to do, I needed to become more familiar with the people's background and values.

As it happened in 1969 we were preparing for a General Chapter (Assembly) the following year. At such gatherings, held every six years, representatives of the Columbans working in different countries come together to discuss ways of meeting new challenges. Some of our men in Japan decided to get the debate going by launching a newsletter and encouraging members to put their ideas down on paper. Seeing it as an opportunity to find out whether others shared my concerns, I wrote an article asking whether the Society was merely a travel agency.

The Society's traditional mode of operation was simple, based on the belief that priests were required to help the new Churches of Asia and Latin America get on their feet. Since the universal Church was the same everywhere, only minor changes had to be made to accommodate non-Western cultures and there was no need for specialised mission training in areas such as civilisations, religions and communicating cross-culturally.

Essentially the Society saw its role as recruiting young men, giving them the basic seven-year clerical training and sending them out to the missions. There the local bishop would place them in a parish where they were needed and give them the necessary guidance. The Society, of course, would continue to support its members there and assist them with their travel home on vacation, health problems and further studies. In short, its services were similar to those offered by competent travel agencies.

In my article I posed the question whether this was enough. Sharing one's deepest convictions is difficult enough in one's own culture, doing so in a completely different culture calls for special training and planning, neither of which was being provided. Was it not time to change our approach? Shouldn't we be setting our own priorities and providing specialised training?

I don't know if my words had any impact, though I was invited to address the Assembly one night when I was in Ireland. However, a strength of the Society was its willingness to support individual members who wanted to do further studies and I decided to avail of the opportunity.

During those final years of my first term in Korea my language ability improved and I was becoming more familiar with the people's thinking and behaviour. What that way of life was based on still eluded me but I had become more attracted to finding the answer. The question posed in Kangjin also needed more attention. What had I got to offer when I finally tuned into the people's wave length? I needed to prepare to be more deeply involved wherever my next spell in Korea took me.

Chapter 3
Unlocking Confucius

On my way back to Ireland in April 1969 I got a round-the-world ticket that would take me via Hong Kong, Bombay and Ethiopia to Ireland and back again to Korea through Canada. It was an opportunity to see the world outside Asia and compare experiences. My interest in alternative approaches to living was about to be broadened.

The original reason for my visit to Ethiopia was to visit my sister, Rosaleen, who was stationed there. However Ethiopia had the oldest Church in Africa and besides seeing my sister I could find out how Christianity had adapted over a period of almost 2,000 years.

The first stop-over was Hong Kong, still a British colony and beginning to make its name as a manufacturing giant. Mainlanders were flocking over the border to escape the worsening situation in Mao's China and grab the low-wage jobs that were fuelling economic growth.

The city was already buzzing with an energy and urgency that, along with its reassuring English street names and convenient transport, made it attractive to Westerners. I did the usual tourist things: walked around Central, crossed on the Star Ferry to the shopping area of Kowloon, went by tram to Victoria Peak and had a seafood meal on a floating restaurant in Aberdeen harbour, still crowded with sampans on which refugees lived.

A visit to the mainland, or even the tense border area, was out of the question and, like most tourists, I was unaware that 40% of Hong Kong is scenic National Park. My inclination to check out the local religious situation was still in its infancy and with no acquaintance there to guide me in the right direction the search was postponed. However, I left feeling I wouldn't mind being part of the city's excitement sometime in the future, never imagining I would be spending seventeen years there at a later stage.

I had a night's stop-over in Bombay, free thanks to Air India at the historic Taj Mahal Hotel which in 2008 was to get world headlines when attacked by terrorists. I arrived in Ethiopia just before Easter. Haile Selassie was still emperor and, with the help of the Orthodox Church and his own Amharic people, in strict control. However there was peace and a sense of growing prosperity in the capital, Addis Abba. I looked forward to seeing the influence of the Ethiopian Orthodox Church on the traditional Holy Week ceremonies. My sister had already been there a number of years in charge of local candidates for her community, the Daughters of Charity, so between her and the young Sisters I would have knowledgeable local guides.

On Holy Thursday we went to St Gabriel's Church in central Addis which was a disappointment. The parish catered to the foreign community and was staffed by Italian priests so the ceremonies were in English and similar to any Western country.

Good Friday was different. We went out of the city to the Cistercian monastery at Mendida where the liturgy was in the Catholic Orthodox style. This included over 15 minutes of prostrations in which the people went face-down on the floor in front of a Cross, got up again and repeated the process another forty or more times. There were two ways of doing the prostrations, either 'kneel down and flop forward' or bow forward from the waist, bending the knees until both hands touch the floor in front of you. In either cases it was strenuous exercise and despite my resolve to follow local practices I gave up after four or five 'bends.'

At another point the people came forward with sticks to beat a bunch of rags representing the devil.

The way graphic symbols had entered naturally into the devotions held my attention and I wondered when Korea would have the confidence and freedom to do something similar.

Mendida is 75 kilometres from Addis and on the trip there we had the company of two delightful young Ethiopian Sisters,

Senkenesh and Hiruth. They laughed as they described life with the Europeans. One day when they were out visiting a village with two Irish Sisters, the village women took them aside and asked them how much it would cost to buy them back from the foreigners.

The final Holy Week ceremony was at a rural chapel in Metcha run by Dutch priests. When we drove into the compound I was amused to see, at a point where two barely discernable tracks crossed, a large sign with the warning, 'Stop! Children crossing!' Even the Dutch in Ethiopia seemed to have a sense of humour.

There, the liturgy reminded me of Korea. It was in traditional Roman style but the singing and active participation gave it life and the ceremony itself is always rich in symbolism.

Ethiopia struck me as being blessed with great natural scenery, attractive people, unique art and a religious tradition going back to the Old Testament. Perched on a high plateau, it enjoys a sunny but temperate climate, sparking clear air and the promise of rich crops. Its women are considered the most beautiful in Africa, a fact attributed to their Semitic roots. Their tapestries celebrated the meeting of Solomon and the Queen of Sheba (Ethiopia) who were regarded as among their ancestors. There were interesting lessons to be learnt from the way Christianity had developed there but studying them would be a life-long task and my future was already committed to Asia.

Before I left Ethiopia I witnessed some of the extreme poverty in the remoter areas, in one village being moved by the children standing around us, too weak to brush off the flies settling on their eyes, but no one could foresee that greater disasters lay ahead. I was to return to Ethiopia in less happy times.

***

The Ireland I came back to in 1969 had hardly changed. The economy was subdued, you could buy a good second-hand car for £500 and get your money back a year later. RTE, the national TV station, had started broadcasting in 1961 but was only beginning to open the country to different values and ways of life. After the freedom we had as missionaries in Korea, the Church in Ireland seemed allergic to change and complacent as the dominant religion. Priests still wore black suits and hats. People questioned why I wore less formal clothing.

I spent the summer with my parents, who were not in good health, reconnecting with relatives and seeing parts of the country I had never visited before. Early in August I was informed that I had been accepted for a course in Mission Science in Ottawa that started on September 1. This created a rush to assemble the necessary papers and when I posted my application for a room in the residence of the university, there was a good chance I would arrive in Ottawa before it.

St Pauls College is part of Ottawa University and within walking distance of the city centre. I did get a room at the College residence and found that most of the lodgers were priests from different parts of Canada. It was a bi-lingual institution but most of the lectures I wanted to attend were in English.

At the time I did not realise how lucky I was to be doing a Mission Science course. Usually people embarking on mission studies end up doing Missiology, the theological investigations of the why and what of mission, drawing on scripture and earlier theological writings. Mission Science was more concerned with the 'how.' This meant courses in the new human sciences of anthropology, community development, world religions, psychology and counselling as well as the theological background of mission.

One day while walking across the leafy square between the university and the residence I met a priest from the eastern province of Nova Scotia. I asked him what he was studying and he said he had just completed his PhD and was preparing his thesis for publication. I enquired as to what the subject was.

'The freedom of the Children of God,' he replied. 'You know, in St Paul's epistles.'

'That's great,' I said, as I already felt the laity should be playing a greater role in the church, 'Is it going to be published in paperback soon for ordinary folk?'

'Paperback?' he asked, sounding somewhat shocked. 'This book is for academics, not ordinary people.'

It gave me an image of academics building a pyramid of knowledge by drawing from the books of other academics, adding their own insights and creating new bricks for the next layer in a limitless structure.

The weather in Ottawa was similar to that of Seoul. Once winter arrived in late October, canals froze over and snow lined the streets. Fortunately both the residence, Maison Deschatelets, and the College were well heated. Each morning I put on my heavy jacket, over-shoes and cap, trudged through the snow across the yard, took off my outer clothing in the college locker room and got down to work.

In my seminary days I had never been an enthusiastic student. I studied enough to pass exams but the subject matter, and the way it was taught, never caught my imagination. We were expected to learn the correct answers and not encouraged to work anything out for ourselves.

In Ottawa I did more study in one year than I had during my seven in the seminary. Going there had not been part of a plan, it had been decided on the spur of the moment, but it prepared the ground for everything I was to do later in Korea and China.

With my list of questions from Korea crying out for attention, I spent most of my time in the library. When we had a choice of doing papers or an exam I knew immediately what I wanted to research while others were wondering what they might write about.

At the end of the first semester, the dean told me I should try for a MA degree rather than settle for the one-year diploma. Keen missionary that I was, I told him I was anxious to get back to Korea the following September. I realised that while studies were unending, the real answers were to be found 'out there.' He told me it was possible to qualify for the MA if I did a few extra courses in the second semester and wrote a formal dissertation which I could defend in September on my way back to Korea. This, in theory, would make it a two year course. I said, 'Why not?'

Two topics that held my attention from the beginning were the relevance of missionary work in today's world and the influence of Confucianism on Korean life. Together they prepared me for the role of 'curious guest' and provided me with the key to finally understanding Korea.

I soon discovered that the study of missionary activity was quite new and the Protestant Churches had been the first to take it seriously. Before that, the purpose of mission had been taken for granted. In the Catholic Church the need to rethink mission was recognised when a Belgian Jesuit, Pierre Charles, stated in 1939 that the most urgent goal was not to save souls but to establish a Church that was capable of taking on the tasks of saving souls. This upset a lot of missionaries whose priority had been baptising adults or babies to save them from eternal separation from God. Building parishes to do this was important but trying to establish a 'Church' that would draw on the traditions and practices of the people and make Christianity easier for them to absorb sounded like a distraction. In Korea I had never heard of Charles or his ideas but they would not have been popular in the wider Church either.

A contemporary of Charles, Alex Glorieux, proposed that mission was not a matter of life or death for pagans but rather a question of 'fullness of life.' This was slow to catch on also.

However the writings of a modern theologian, Karl Rahner, on 'anonymous Christians' were attracting attention and could not be ignored. Rahner held that God had the welfare of all people at heart and if people lived according to their conscience and the teachings of their own religion, they could be saved. He agreed that Christianity had the 'fullness of life' and deep down everyone was looking for the good news it transmitted but if, through no fault of their own, truth-seeking people were not baptised they could at least be considered 'anonymous Christian' and achieve union with God.

I had heard Ranher being quoted to prove there was no longer any need for missionary work and at last I had a chance to find out what he actually said. The recent Vatican Council opened up discussion by admitting that baptism was not necessary for salvation. In doing so it deflated the enthusiasm of many deeply committed missionaries with the dramatic results that can still be felt today. Previously the motivation had been simple, 'Missionaries save souls,' but if souls could be saved without the Church where was the urgency? Why give your life to it? These questions were to trouble many for years to come.

The paper I wrote on my research ended with a description of what I hoped to do myself when I returned to Korea but in it I was also not slow to tell others what they should be doing.

The advice I had for theologians was not to rely solely on academic research but to value the experience of missionaries 'in the field'; to take social, cultural and economic factors into consideration and be wary of spreading theories without thought of their effect on missionary motivation. I had experienced how academics could cause confusion by being out of touch with what was actually happening.

For missionaries, I suggested that quality was more important than numbers, a timetable should be set for the establishment of Churches on the lines Charles described, and it was important to know the 'silent language' of the people–their culture, religious heritage and social problems. Maybe my thinking was a bit ahead of what was possible in missionary circles at that time and I was falling into the academic trap myself.

In Ottawa I was able to catch up with recent missionary developments but keeping up with them was obviously going to be an on-going challenge. However, there was one area in which I could make immediate progress and that was in Confucianism. I had encountered it as a living reality in Korea and wanted to discover how it managed to dominate the daily lives of millions of people over millennia. Fortunately the college had an excellent section on Oriental Studies.

Though hundreds of volumes have been written about Confucianism, its 'sacred books' are not philosophical speculations but a collection of anecdotes and examples drawn from the life and teachings of the scholar Confucius and his disciples. At first reading there does not seem to be any order or connection in the stories but eventually I discovered a key to making them intelligible.

When reading Paul S. Crane's book on what is unique in Korean life, I was impressed by the way he pinpointed the 'patterns' of behaviour which were followed in different situations. If a person embarrassed themselves in public by doing something foolish or wrong, they would just smile. Westerners reacted to this in surprise because an expression of regret was what they expected. Crane explained, 'That is just what they always do in such a situation,' but he didn't try to say why.

I was interested in finding out the 'why' and got a clue when reading Ruth Benedict's, *The Chrysanthemum and the Sword*. Benedict was an American anthropologist asked by the US military, when they occupied Japan after World War ll, to help them understand the Japanese mind which was totally unfamiliar to them. Two of the key elements in the Japanese psyche which she highlighted were *'giri'* and *'gimu.'* The two words are related, one means the 'principle of *gi*' and the other the 'practice of *gi*.'

She explained that *gi* was a Confucian virtues that meant 'duty.' This sense of responsibility was so strong among Japanese that a kamikaze pilot was willing to crash his plane into a ship to destroy it and a defeated soldier would commit suicide by hari-kiri rather than surrender.

On reading this I remembered hearing of 'Five Basic Virtues' in Confucianism. I checked the original wording in Chinese characters and found that, sure enough, *gi* was one of them. In Korean it was pronounced *oui* as in *oui-ri* and *oui-mu*, and in Chinese, *yi* as in *yi-li* and *yi-mu*.

If *gi* was so important in defining the Japanese temperament, I wondered what influence the other 'Basic Virtues' had on the Korean, Chinese and Japanese character. Could they help explain the 'patterns of behaviour' described by Crane? Was this the clue I had being looking for?

Excited by the prospect, I went through the basic books of Confucianism looking for the five virtues and how they were practiced. In doing so I began to appreciate the genius of Confucius himself and why his message still dominates social life in Asia.

Confucius insisted that he did not create anything new, he just recorded what he considered the fundamentals of Chinese life and gave examples from historical figures. Running consistently through all his stories were a number of key 'virtues' or concepts which he believed expressed the best of human nature. Tradition fixed the number as five.

I had heard about some of those concepts in my language studies but they had meant little to me at the time. Now, viewing them as a unit, interacting and building on each other, I could see how they made sense. They explained why the people had acted in ways that puzzled me because they were different or even the opposite of what Westerners would do in similar circumstances. My Masters dissertation was based on this insight and I enjoyed the challenge of filling in the details.

Ottawa also offered an introduction to topics with which I was less familiar. We studied world religions under an American professor, John A Hardon SJ. His approach was to compare the major religions by listing them under a set of categories such as deity, world view, worship, salvation, prayer, scriptures and morality. I would have preferred to hear what each religion meant in practice to its adherents but at least it was an opportunity to do some background study. Shamanism, in which I was also interested, was not on the list.

Buddhism is another key element in the Korean heritage but beyond learning about the different schools it was not the time or place to explore it more deeply.

Psychiatry was a new field for me. The professor was known for the clarity of his lectures and his very strict marking. Taking the chance that it might ruin my run of straight 'A's, I joined his course feeling that some knowledge of the field would help me in understanding the Korean mind.

During his first lecture he stated he was no longer a practising Catholic himself and the paper he set for us was, 'Religion is an obstacle in achieving a mature personality.' We were free to write for or against this topic but I was confident that the marking, however strict, would not depend of which side we favoured. In any case, I passed.

Because of my passion for the subjects I was studying, my time in Ottawa went quickly. At weekends I walked the snow-packed sidewalks towards Parliament Hill with its tall French architecture reflected in the icy river. We sometimes played a form of ice hockey on the frozen Rideau Canal which did not melt till early May. 'English' Ottawa was still a conservative city and to see a movie on Sunday we had to cross the river to the 'French' or Catholic city of Hull in Quebec.

I went back to Ireland in the early summer to have my dissertation typed up formally. It was based on the Confucian virtues as a key to understanding the Asian mentality and I gave it the title, 'The Practice of the Confucian Social Ideal.' However, since my course was 'Mission Science' I had to tie it in with a missionary theme. My solution was to entitle it, 'The Confucian Social Ideal: A Prerequisite for the Missionary's Understanding of Oriental Society.'

This was acceptable to Professor Hardon who understood my reluctance to rewrite the whole manuscript and I just had to add a new final chapter to accommodate the change in direction. However, in September when it came to defending the dissertation on my way back to Korea, I was asked to explain why a knowledge of Confucianism was necessary. The examiner in question must have noticed that the content did not exactly line up with the chosen title but my impromptu explanation was accepted. An understanding of Confucianism is essential for anyone working in the Orient, though many excellent missionaries never got around to studying it.

That summer, while I was completing my dissertation in Ireland, I was asked to talk about my studies to the members of our General Chapter, then in session at our college at Dalgan Park. This was the meeting for which I had submitted a paper inquiring whether the Society was just a travel agency, moving priests around the world, or a missionary organisation with its own vision and strategies.

I gave the Assembly a report on the emerging social sciences and the ideas of Charles and Rahner on mission. It was the first major meeting of our Society after Vatican II and the members were grappling with its implications for Church and mission. Discussions between traditionalists and progressives became so intense that the allotted time had to be extended. It took over four months to complete.

A document eventually emerged that addressed the new challenges: dialogue with other religions, justice, labour unions, youth, China, communications, local vocations and lay mission. Cultural adaptation, however, was barely mentioned. It was one of the best documents the Society produced but it would take many years for the ideas to sink in. The structural changes it called for inspired little enthusiasm.

At the informal gathering at which I spoke, I was asked what I thought of recent developments in Korea, especially the 'urban apostolate' being promoted by our new Director. With rapid industrial development families were surging into the cities and the Director had bought parcels of land in the Seoul suburbs and was looking for men to build parishes there. This is what he was referring to as the 'urban apostolate.'

Perhaps too bluntly I replied that if the men going to run parishes in the city operated on the same lines as they had in rural areas, it could hardly be called an 'urban apostolate.' I was thinking of the efforts being made in Canada to bring a new approach to the grim realities of impoverished inner-city districts. We Columbans were still a long way from such thinking. The Director understandably was not too impressed by my retort and shortly afterwards when I took on one of those new developments myself he was probably watching to see just what I would do that was different.

In September 1970, full of new ideas and enthusiasm, I finished my round-the-world trip by taking a plane from Ottawa back to a Korea that had changed even more than I had.

Chapter 4
Marketplace Immersion

D uring my year's absence, President Park Chung-hee's Second Five Year Plan was revolutionising Korea. That July the motorway between Seoul in the north and the vital southern port of Busan had been completed, cutting travel time by half. It no longer took most of the day to travel on bad roads from Kunsan to Kangjin.

Park had been an army general before leading a coup in 1961 and he understood the importance of infrastructure. Following the example of Japan in becoming an industrial power he began with road networks, electricity grid, waterworks and phone communications. The First Plan had concentrated on establishing labour-intensive textile manufacturing and encouraged young people to move into Seoul from the countryside. Now the emphasis was on middle and heavy industry and whole families were moving into the cities.

For me it was the best possible time to return. I was not short of ideas and confidence after Ottawa and the ideal place to start would be somewhere completely new with no limiting traditions set by previous pastors.

Soon after my return the vice-Director took me on a tour of the 'new Seoul.' The city was spreading at a remarkable rate. In an article I wrote at that time, I said you only had to stand still to see it pass out beyond you. Fortunately the Columbans had received a large bequest from the States and spent it on five plots of land in the growing suburbs. Four of them had already been allotted to former parish priests and I was offered the last and least developed.

It was located in what was then countryside beside the Seoul Country Club, the only golf course in the city besides that on the US base. Already there were plans to close the club and reopen it as a Children's Park. The area was known as Hwa Yang Village (*Ni*) and all it had was a marketplace and cluster of shops near a crossroads with the beginnings of a residential development.

The vice-Director knew only two Catholics in the area but with the way it was growing he was sure the numbers would grow quickly. He showed me the site he had bought, it was less than half of a mile from the village centre and already a few houses were being built near it. He added that if the site was found unsuitable we could move to a better one. For me it was ideal.

First, negotiations with the neighbouring parishes and the diocese had to be completed so I took the opportunity to sign up for a three-month language course at our old language school. It was the sixth and final semester of the program we had begun in 1965 so I had a sense of finishing my formal language studies. However, mastering Korean would be a life project.

During those months preparations for Hwa-yang Ni began. One of the two Catholics we knew there was my old language teacher, Seo Chong-su. He was now a lecturer in a nearby university and lived close to the village with his mother, wife and three children. He seemed as excited as me in getting something new off to a good start.

We began looking around for a temporary church and found space in an almost-completed two-storey concrete building near the crossroads. It was designed for commercial use with sliding glass windows on the upper floor and when we left it a year later it reverted to what it was originally intended to be, a pool hall. Underneath it were a wine shop, a restaurant, a comic book reading room and a dry cleaner. The stairs up to our 'church' shared an entrance with the wine shop which surprised those of our visitors who presumed all Christians were anti-alcohol.

We fixed 8 November 1970 as our opening day and asked the neighbouring parishes to inform people living in the Hwa Yang area to come to our marketplace church on that date.

An hour before the opening I walked around our 'church' wondering how many people would turn up. Seo Chong-su's mother, dressed simply like the rural grandmother she was with a towel wrapped around her head, was there with a bucket and mop washing the floor that the builders had just finished. They hadn't completed the job however and there was a hole in the corner waiting for pipes to be inserted. The old lady found it a convenient place to get rid of the dirty water. Unfortunately it was just above the drycleaners and there was a screech from below that alerted both of us to the fact that something was not right. I could hear the lady from the dry cleaners come thumping up the stairs and cowardly turned aside to let the grandmother face her wrath. My language was not yet up to full speed and we hadn't reached the chapter on 'How to deal with angry neighbours.'

The dry cleaner lady worked off her displeasure with a five minute tirade and then retreated down the stairs muttering about mad foreigners and mad grandmothers from the countryside. It was not an auspicious start but from then on things looked up.

About forty people arrived, shopkeepers from the marketplace, men engaged in the building trade and a few local residents like Seo Chong-su and his family. After Mass we signed up seven of the men to form a parish council, one of the first in Seoul. They were all in favour of spending a year in the temporary quarters, collecting money and seeing if there was a better site than the one picked by the vice-Director. Some had only primary school education and one was a professor but they got on well together from the first day and remained the main support for the parish, and me, for the next four years.

From the beginning the enthusiasm was infectious. We made plans to block off a corner of the floor area for my living/dining/office room and a tiny kitchen. I moved in before Christmas, still not believing my luck.

Four years later, when I was about to leave Hwa Yang Ni, I wrote a book about the people there.

I called it *The Scrutable Oriental* which caused my Korean publishers to scratch their heads over their English dictionaries.

'There is no such word as "scrutable",' they said. They knew the word 'inscrutable' and had probably heard the expression 'inscrutable Oriental' though they never told me what they thought about that. However, I wanted to show there was a simple way of understanding the Oriental mind and 'scrutable' had to be the opposite of 'inscrutable.'

The book was based on my dissertation on the 'Five Confucian Virtues' I had researched in Ottawa and I dedicated it to, 'The people of Hwa Yang Ni, Seoul, who were the atmosphere, the stimulus and the material for this book.' In fact it was a collection of articles I wrote for the 'Thoughts of the Times' in the English-language *The Korea Times* over those four years.

In thirty-four chapters I related how familiarity with the five virtues had helped me grasp what was going on around me in Hwa Yang Ni and why people acted in ways that once appeared strange.

Besides articles on the virtues themselves, there were such diverse chapters as the Ideal Man, the Ideal Woman, Nothing for Nothing, the Picnic Problem, the Compact Home, Education Complexes, Face, Symbols of New Korea, The Role of Alcohol, Born Entrepreneurs, Deference to the Unknown, Suicidal Mosquitoes and Harmony with the Universe.

The ideal Confucian gentleman is called *kun-ja* in Korean and one of the five civil divisions in my new parish was *Kun-ja* District. I took this as a good omen.

Early on, as Hwa Yang Ni began to take the shape of a settled residential area, a family moved in that gave more prestige to the church. The father had been the ambassador to a North African country and previous to that, commander of the Korean Marine Corps. He was between postings and turned out to be a good example of a *kun-ja*.

Every Sunday he came to Mass in our church-above-the-wine-house with his wife, son and four daughters. Because of his diplomatic life they had spent many years abroad. His son and two of the girls had attended English speaking schools and two went to French schools. After Mass the two English-speaking girls would talk with me while their father chatted with the members of the parish council. He could not be involved directly in parish activities as it would not help his diplomatic career to be closely associated with a Church already critical of the government, but he allowed his name to be listed as an honorary council member. He paid the highest amount of monthly donations though his wife had reservations since they were not as rich as might seem.

One day he invited me to his house and I went, expecting a relaxed family meal. However only his wife and son were with him and after a simple tea-and-fruit respite his wife left the room. The ambassador then straightened himself, paused for a moment and proceeded to tell me about his son's shortcomings, how he was wasting his time and not settling down and getting married. The son, in his early thirties, sat there quietly with his head bowed.

When he had finished, the father then turned to me and said, 'Father, please give him advice and tell him to do his duty.'

For a moment I was speechless. Here was a man who had previously been an army general asking me, a foreigner, to counsel his grown-up son in front of him. I was amazed at his humility, and confidence in me.

Then it struck me that this was what a true *kun-ja* would do.

Around that time I wrote about the *kun-ja* in a *Korea Times* article.

'Those who have been around the Far East for a while know what the *kun-ja* looks like. He is well groomed and reserved, careful to show respect for others, to see himself in their eyes and to make adjustments accordingly. He runs his family or business, not by loud authority, but quietly by the weight of respect his self-control and dignity demand. He has probably developed a strong affection for his wife but he will not reveal it in public. Only in strict privacy will he talk to her freely and treat her almost as an equal. Nor do his relations with his children hint that they are his greatest pride and consolation. Sometimes he might long to take them in his arms and show them his love but always he manages to resist the temptation because such behaviour might weaken his ability to command respect, not only for himself, but for all authority and ultimately for order in society.'

This description came not from academic study but from people I got to know, like the ambassador, but the classics did spell out the details.

Confucius said, 'From the Emperor down to the common people all must consider the cultivation of the person as the root of society,' and impressively, the ordinary people of Hwa Yang Ni took this seriously. They might not always be able to act as *kun-jas* but they knew they should be.

Confucius went on to state, 'Govern the people by laws and regulate them by penalties and they will try to do no wrong but they will lose the sense of shame. Govern the people by virtue and restrain them by rules of propriety and the people will have a sense of shame and be reformed by themselves.' I thought, this should be the outlook of Christians too.

Describing the *kun-ja* he said, '*Kun-ja* presents three different aspects. On first look he appears stern and forbidding. On close acquaintance he becomes gentle and mild, and when he has to speak in public he becomes firm and decisive.'

This behaviour is part of the five virtue system. The ambassador's basic concern for his son came from the first Confucian virtue, *Ren* in Chinese.

Confucius defined it as, 'Love due to men,' and this included women and children because *Ren* begins in the family. According to him, 'I treat the aged in my family and extend this to the aged in other men's families; I treat the young in my family properly and extend this to the young in other men's families.'

I was brought into the ambassador's family discussion because of the second virtue, *Yi*. The Chinese, long before Confucius, realised that the ideal of universal love was impractical. It had to begin with those close to you and, if circumstances allowed, it should be extended to those with whom you have bonds. They listed the five main bonds as: father-son, husband-wife, between brothers, between friends and between those in authority and those under them.

Ever practical, they stressed the responsibilities that come with each relationship. This sense of duty is called *Yi*, pronounced *Gi* in Japanese and given prominence as such in Ruth Benedict's book on the Japanese mind, *The Chrysanthemum and the Sword*. It also explains why Korean is a difficult language to learn—the words and verb endings you use must show the level of respect due to the person you are talking to or about.

In the ambassador's family, the father's sense of responsibility to his son was causing him anxiety. The eldest son in Oriental families seems to be spoilt and get the best of everything but some day he will have to settle down and take on financial and other responsibilities towards his parents, siblings, cousins and anyone else related to him.

The ambassador looked on me as a 'Spiritual Father' and teacher in the church so I too had a duty towards his son and he took it for granted that I had the requisite wisdom to go with those roles.

The third virtue, *Li,* was about ritual and determined the way in which the meeting was arranged. Again the pragmatic Chinese had decided that there should be fixed ways of showing the correct degree of respect due to others.

Our interview was held in a formal setting, the father presented his request with humility, using the correct level of formal language and confessing his own shortcomings. His son listened obediently and offered no excuses. Finally it came time for the 'wise teacher' to be 'firm and decisive,' a responsibility I felt was beyond me.

There is an expression in Korean for what is usually said on such occasions. It is *'choen-malsum'* and means 'fine words.' Usually these are generalisations such as stressing the importance of 'duty,' 'obedience' and 'responsibility' and make up for having nothing personal to say. I avoid them if possible but on that occasion, to my embarrassment, I might have succumbed.

While the last two of the Confucian virtues are Wisdom and Sincerity, I felt I lacked the necessary 'wisdom' while wishing 'sincerely' to be of help.

I walked away from the house with some awe for what I had witnessed. I recognised I had more to learn from the ambassador than his son had to learn from me. His humility and sense of duty were beyond what we are used to in the West and I wondered what it would take to make me follow his example.

***

After a year in the market place, we moved to a disused factory about four hundred metres away. During that time the parish council examined one possible site after another until I became an expert on land values in the area. Our preference from the beginning was a low hill, the only high ground in what had not so long ago been flat rice paddies. It was at the edge of the old village and the dilapidated building on it was classified as a royal pavilion.

The local real-estate agents, picturesquely called 'Luck and Virtue Room men,' assured us they could get the classification changed but we eventually ran out of patience. Those modest buildings still stand untouched on the hillock today.

Our next preference was an empty factory near the new crossroads to the south of the village. We could afford to buy only half of it. The front, since it was more accessible, would be more expensive so we settled for the rear.

One evening we invited the Columban Regional Council to view the site and they were not too enthusiastic. Some were dubious about the number of locals who accompanied us, parish councils were not common in Seoul in those days, while others maintained that, 'They had never before heard of a successful transformation of a factory into a church.' Eventually we got their approval.

Our half of the factory included a manager's residence and a gatehouse. The residence was a flimsy tile-fronted two-storey building, the top floor becoming my dwelling while we used the lower for classes and meetings. The gatehouse came in handy as a parish office.

With the money we had already collected we refurbished our half-factory for use as a church that could hold three hundred people. To raise its profile in the neighbourhood we added a concrete bell tower. The tower was seven storeys high and designed by a professor of engineering in Han Yang University who had just moved into the area. After I left Hwa Yang Ni, the Columban who followed me had the factory building knocked and replaced with a purpose-built concrete structure and his successor, a Korean priest, knocked that in turn and built another new church. However the tower proudly remains.

By the time of our move the number of parishioners had increased to almost one thousand. They were nearly all newcomers to the area and once they found the church they gave me a sketched map of where they lived. Street numbers in Seoul are not in sequence and No 3 could be beside No 75 as they were allotted on a first-come first-served basis. As soon as possible I would set out with a district leader to visit the family. With the areas developing so fast sometimes there was no district leader yet so I would appoint the first likely candidate I met and continue the visits with her. All the district leaders were women as they were freer in the daytime and had less problem visiting homes where there were only women present.

Community was very important to the newcomers who had recently moved in from rural villages. Organising them according to districts under a district leader met some of their needs but we also started a number of 'societies,' called *hui* in Korean. We had the Mothers Society, the Young Adults Society, the choir, the Students society, the Young Christian Workers, the Legion, St Andrew Kim Society (for older couples) and the St John Society (for younger couples) as well as the Funeral Society and the St Paul Society. Fortunately they met on a monthly rather than a weekly basis.

The Funeral Society had deep roots in Korean tradition. The members took care of funeral arrangements, prayed with the families, got them a plot in a Catholic cemetery and led the liturgy.

I made the mistake of going out to the graveyard with my first funeral, to give the blessing there. The Funeral Society seemed unimpressed at the idea which should have been a warning. It was only when I got there that I realised they were used to doing the whole ceremony on their own.

They checked the grave to see it was properly aligned according to the rules of geomancy, arguing loudly whether the coffin should be pointing more to the left or right to insure the happiness of the deceased and the family left behind. The length and intensity of the discussions demonstrated the extent of their knowledge of the rules and the importance of getting it right.

They sang the litany and prayers, alternating in a steady drone in the Buddhist style. Whether this went back directly to a Buddhist tradition or even earlier I could not discover. From that one visit to the graveyard I learnt that that funeral practices are sacred and best left in the hands of those most familiar with them.

The Funeral Society also played a big role in bringing new families to the church. Often when a non-Catholic neighbour was close to dying someone from the Funeral Society would visit to console them and talk about the advantages of having faith. If the patient wanted it, they would then baptise him or her and hold the funeral in the Catholic tradition. The families were so grateful they would often come to the Church afterwards and request baptism.

Even though we did not have a good introductory course for newcomers entering the Church the numbers multiplied and we founded the St Paul Society to help them settle into their new life as Christians. They were delighted to hear that Paul was a latecomer in following Christ and would be a good model for those baptised as adults. It became very popular and made up in some way for the limitations of our methods of instruction.

Our first instructor was a tiny but determined lady who turned up at our first Mass. She claimed she had taught catechumens in a nearby parish and within a week she had her first class going. However I found her teaching, though enthusiastic, was limited and when we decided to employ a fulltime office man I looked for someone who would be both a good example and an effective teacher.

Bundo (Benedict) Ko was recommended to me by a colleague. He had just retired from being a warder at the infamous West Gate Prison in Seoul. There he had taken on the role of preparing those awaiting execution who showed an interest in being baptised. A month after he came to work with us he approached me one morning looking sad. He informed me that twelve of his 'godsons' had been executed the previous day and another eight would be executed that day.

The parishioners came to like and admire him but he turned out to be neither a great teacher nor a public speaker. Fortunately I had a number of articulate and enthusiastic young men who had moved into the area to work at managerial level in nearby electronic factories such as Motorola. They were in their thirties and once co-opted into the parish council they organised all our activities and celebrations. Their wives too were well educated and outgoing. A generation later they might have occupied important roles in business or government themselves but fortunately for me at that time they were busy looking after their homes and helping their neighbours. As couples they generated great energy when they came together in a *hui* but they were also active as district leaders and in the choir or Mothers Society.

A group that brought a different element to our parish life was the Young Christian Workers. They had been meeting in the area before our parish started but gathered in our church once I showed an interest in their activities. The YCW, for short, was founded in France to extend the 'see, judge, act' Christian program to work places. In our branch all the members were women in their twenties who worked on machines in local textile, wig or watch factories. The union movement had started in Korea but the authorities were determined to limit its development as much as possible. In fact most factories had no union and anyone who mentioned the word was seen as a potential troublemaker and could soon lose their job.

Union involvement was not a YCW priority but as an organisation concerned about workers conditions and rights it was bound to get involved. The members were a lively group who ran their own meetings, keeping me informed on some of the developments. I encouraged them to join with the university students who taught in our Sunday School to organise night classes for workers seeking to further their education.

The night school quickly became popular. It used the church as a school room and soon twenty to thirty workers attended, many from the wig factory next door. This fact was soon brought to my attention by the local representative of the Security Bureau.

He called to the office one day and Bundo apprehensively escorted him to my upstairs residence. The policeman announced that the wig factory was going to stop its workers from attending our night school as it was interfering with their work. He added that the school had a bad influence with its pro-union and Marxist agenda. He suggested that we close it. Coming from the much-feared Security Bureau, that sounded serious.

I told him, as any good Korean would, that I would think about it. I had once been advised by an elderly parishioner, 'Father, if you have to say "No" to some proposal, just say, "I'll think about it," and that will make everyone happy.'

The following evening there was a larger crowd than usual at the night school when the police raided it, filling the yard as well as the church. They started questioning both teachers and students, taking their names and addresses and asking them where they studied or worked. The teachers, who were university students, were intimidated as their future studies could be under threat. Since I had invited them to get involved I thought l should do something about it.

The next morning I asked Bundo to contact the district office of the Security Bureau and arrange a meeting with the man in charge. He thought I was out of my mind to put my head into the lion's den; everyone knew you should avoid the Security Bureau as much as possible.

The District Office was in Ku-I Dong, the neighbouring area, and I walked over there in the afternoon. I raised some eyebrows in the reception area when I asked for the head of the Security Section but was finally ushered to his office. He was an average-sized man, in his forties, dressed in civvies and appeared friendly.

I told him that there had been some misunderstanding and explained that we were providing a community service in the spirit of President Park's 'New Community' movement calling on everyone to work together for the nation. The volunteer teachers in the night school were university students and their parents would be alarmed if they heard the Security Bureau had something against them.

He did not seem to be well briefed on the situation and asked me to sit down and drink some tea while he summoned the Hwa Yang Ni officer. The man in question could not be found so he called in one of his assistants and asked me to tell them what had happened. They listened carefully and then spoke about the situation in Korea and how business people were doubtful about labour unions as they were often infiltrated by pro-North Korean communists. They then asked me about myself, where I came from and how long I had I been in the country.

Finally the section head asked in a confidential tone, 'Seriously, what do you really think of the situation in Korea today?'

I repeated what I has said about our hopes to be of service to our local comunity, using the government approved text books in our night school. I also mentioned that I had once worked in the Vatican Embassy and knew the Superintendent Choi who was killed when the North Koreans attacked the Blue House. Finally I said, 'If we supress freedom here just as they do in the North, what difference will there be?'

The two men coughed uncomfortably. I then asked the Chief, in a similar confidential tone, 'But seriously, what do you think of the situation?'

He straightened up and proceeded to give me the official line about strengthening the economy and holding back the communists. As we parted he gave me his name card and told me he would see the officer for Hwa Yang Ni and clear up the matter.

I was in the middle of my breakfast the following morning when the officer in question thumped on the door and came in very apologetically. He wanted to know why I had bothered the Section Chief about such a small matter. The wig factory has removed all its objections and would do everything it could to ensure its workers could attend. If there were any problems in the future, I was not to go to the Section Chief but just contact him and all would be solved.

He was no sooner out the door than the lady manager of the wig factory appeared. She regretted that she had never called on me before and that this misunderstanding had occurred. She thought the night school was a great idea and they might even start one themselves. I offered her some tea and assured her we would be good neighbours in the future.

Occasionally after that I would see the Section Chief in a local restaurant. We would bow to each other across the room. His card came in useful when dealing with other local policemen who came to bother me with long forms to be filled out. All I had to say was, 'How is my good friend Section Chief Kim in the Security Bureau?' They would pause and say, 'You know him?' and quickly take their leave.

In fact, our support for the workers was about the only thing we did to reach out into the local community. Hwa Yang Ni was an expanding middle class area so there were few poor people besides the young factory workers lodging there. I had hoped to be more involved in local affairs but Church and officialdom seldom met at that time. It was harder for foreigners who did not know how the system worked and had few chances to meet local officials unless they came to the church. It was only later, in Shillim 10, that I was able to overcome the barriers.

**

Korea was changing. The light industry encouraged by President Park's Five Year Plan created jobs and gave a degree of prosperity to people not afraid of hard work and who valued education. One of the last articles I wrote before leaving Hwa Yang Ni was a reflection on the 'Born Entrepreneurs' I met on a daily basis.

It hadn't taken me long to notice what seemed to be a contradiction in the culture. The people adapted quickly to any sort of business opportunity but in Confucian circles commerce was looked down on, scholarly activities taking preference.

Mencius, the most famous follower of Confucius, found that when he visited one state after another he was always asked by the ruler, 'How can your teaching profit my state?' Mencius' reply was that if the king asked, 'How can I profit my state?' the ministers will ask, 'How can we profit our estates?' and the nobles and commoners will ask, 'How can we profit ourselves?' Thus individuals would compete with each other for profit and all men suffer as a result. Mencius stated, 'I have come to teach the *Ren* (good relationships) and *Yi* (duties due to social position) of Confucius. If these flourish, the King and all his people will prosper. Please do not speak of profit.'

Since then, commerce was seen as the lowest occupation with scholars, military and farmers taking precedence.

This tradition remains very much in the hearts and minds of the people in China, Korea, Japan and other countries in East Asia. Their devotion to education is one result. Already primary school students were going to 'study institutes' on a daily basis to get in extra hours before the next exam, with the ultimate goal of getting into university. Even in the tiny shared rooms of squatter areas, the younger members of the family concentrated on their books under a weak electric bulb till 2.00 am.

When speaking to, or about a teacher, honorific terms had to be used and meeting a person with a Doctorate would make one's day. We had two professors, Seo Chong-su and the Engineering Professor who designed our bell tower, so together with our ambassador, they added some distinction to our community.

On the other hand Koreans, like many others in Asia, seem to have a natural talent for business. If a lower government official lost his job for any reason he would not think twice about opening a 'hole-in-the wall' shop selling sweets and a few basic items. If that went well he would expand the business and if he went bankrupt he would just move to another area and start all over again.

In the Ku-I Dong area I often called into the house of one of our area leaders. The home was small, with three rooms and an outside toilet, but the tiny yard behind it was covered over with plastic sheets and a steady hum of an engine came from it. Her husband, who was not a Catholic then, proudly showed me the machine he had installed there. It produced the tiny bulbs that are used as warning lamps in computers and other electronic devices. Thousands of them, different in size and shape, were heaped around the shed.

Not long afterwards he bought a small factory outside the city and moved his machinery there. By now he is probably a millionaire running a large electrical appliance company.

Every family seemed to be involved in one or more *kyes*. A *kye* was formed when a number of people, usually friends or neighbours, came together monthly with an economic project in mind. They each contributed a fixed sum to a common fund and took turns in speculating or using it for 30 days. At the end of the month they were expected to return the sum and it would be given to the person whose turn was next.

Of course there were times when the borrower could not return the cash and this could lead to the *kye* breaking up. These informal cooperatives were very useful when people needed a 'lump sum' but more often than not they closed with bad feelings and someone falling into serious debt.

There was also a social element involved, *kyes* giving people a reason to gather regularly. When Ku-I Dong developed, two families moved in who had previously attended a downtown parish. There twelve couples had gathered in a *kye* they called 'The Twelve Apostles' and even when some of them moved out to other places, like Ku-I Dong, they would meet once a month in the local parish, attend Mass there and then go to that member's house for lunch and business.

The first time I was invited to attend I walked to the house with Bundo after the midday Mass. I asked him how much the *kye* was worth. He mentioned a large sum, the equivalent of several thousand US dollars. It seemed the members seldom availed of their right to borrow but added to it every month. When I enquired as to why they kept the *kye* going if they did not use the money, he said it was for *chin-mok*, friendship.

When we got to the house I was surprised to find we were the first guests to arrive. The host was a bank manager and in the Korean style after I had been seated on the floor he handed me a small glass and poured Johnny Walker whisky into it, holding the bottle in both hands.

As usual there were *an-ju* snacks prepared to off-set the alcohol so, even though it was the middle of the day, one drink seemed permissible. However as each couple arrived and sat down, the new guest would find an empty glass and pour me another Scotch. The problem was that I had to empty the glass before filling it and offering it back, using both hands as a sign of respect. With eleven of them coming, each offering a glass that I could not refuse, it was one of the more memorable meals.

***

With the improving economic situation the country was much more confident and enterprising than when I was in Jeju. Most of the families that moved into Hwa Yang Ni came from the countryside with hopes and ambitions for their future but had to struggle for a number of years before finding their place in the city. Churches provided a supporting community and the people had little trouble accepting the Christian worldview and morality.

The concept of One Heavenly God, *Ha-nu-nim,* was familiar to all Koreans and their Confucianism made them attentive to nature's plan for humans as expressed in traditional wisdom such as the Five Virtues. The Christian version of their Heavenly God appeared more compassionate than previously supposed and seemed less like a remote and strict Confucian parent. The Christian Heavenly Father forgave transgressions more easily but might also inflict retribution in serious matters. His sense of strict justice demanded that one performed one's duties or *Yi* with sincerity.

Another reason the Korean people accepted the Catholic Church so readily was the way it had entered their country. It was not completely foreign.

In 1779, a prominent Confucian scholar named Yi Byeok gathered some of his closest friends at a temple near his home south of Hwa Yang Ni to discuss new ideas smuggled into the country through China. The government had a 'Hermit Kingdom' policy to exclude foreign people and teachings in the hope of preserving peace and the status quo.

Yi Byeok had come across a copy of Matteo Ricci's 'True Teaching of the Lord of Heaven' written for Confucian scholars in China. Since it was written in Chinese characters he had no trouble reading it in the original and began sharing his reflections with his friends. They came to the conclusion that it was superior to Buddhism and Taoism and to get more information they asked a young scholar, Yi Seung-hun, who was about to accompany his father to Beijing on the annual diplomatic mission, to find out what he could about the Church.

In the Chinese capital, Yi Seung-hun went immediately to the North Church and began discussions with the French missionaries there. Before he returned home he was baptised, taking the name Peter, and given written materials and religious goods. Yi Byeok and his friends pored over the books and after careful consideration said they were convinced. Yi Seung-hun baptised Yi Byeok, giving him the name 'John the Baptist' in recognition of the role he had played.

Foreign priests did not arrive for another fifty years and in the meantime the Korean Church took on a life of its own. The scholars appointed people from among themselves as bishops and priests and held their own liturgies. One such gathering in a city centre mansion was raided by the police who thought they had come across a gambling den. They were embarrassed to find the house full of nobles and scholars reading books. However the secret was out and persecutions began which went on for over a hundred years.

Despite the intensity of the opposition the Church continued to grow and when French missionaries were eventually smuggled into the country they found believers scattered over the countryside in Catholic villages. In 1984, 103 of the Korean martyrs from that period were canonised in Rome.

This unique story of how the Church came to Korea has been told in films and made into a TV drama series so is well known in the country. Both Catholics and non-Catholics take pride in it. It makes up to some degree for Christianity's foreign image and failure to draw enough on the Korean spiritual heritage, though some traditional practices are incorporated in Lunar New Year and Autumn Festival celebrations.

The people could immediately feel at home in many aspects of Church life. They liked the solemnity of the Mass, comparing it favourably with the noisy and informal celebrations in other Churches. The hierarchical structure with its Pope, bishops and celibate priesthood also appealed to their Confucian sense of order. Indeed they hold their priests in high regard and spoil them unashamedly. I was less optimistic about the shelf life of formality and the stress on uniformity.

Parishioners' financial support was astonishing. During my first two months in the marketplace 'upper room' I got my monthly living expenses from the Columbans but after that the people took on the responsibility and I had no monetary worries there or elsewhere during my time in Korea, even when it came to building programs.

Hwa Yang Ni was my first parish and the only one I started from scratch. When we were setting up our factory church we had to decide on a saint as our patron. I suggested Christ the King as the gospel message of The Kingdom had been on my mind since Kangjin. Some of the women would have preferred Our Lady or a saint's name but already the majority had an idea of what the Kingdom was about and they agreed.

We didn't actually create a perfect Kingdom 'of peace, love and justice' in our neighbourhood. We seldom reached out beyond our own membership to mingle with others and see how we could help them. We were too busy welcoming newcomers and in our growing middle class area there were not many in dire need. I would come more in contact with the realities of poverty in Haeng Dang Dong and Shillim 10. However we did try to keep the ideal of the Kingdom alive through the YCW, the night school and occasional events for the elderly in the area.

I left Hwa Yang Ni on 16 February 1975 and the emotional strains of leaving a Korean parish are not something I could cope with too often in my life. Westerners may regard Asians as 'inscrutable' and unemotional but the facade is there to prevent their very deep feelings from showing and perhaps causing discord in the community. While the *kun-ja* 'Perfect Gentleman' is reluctant to appear upset by anything, deep emotion and sincerity are highly valued.

For over four years I had been immersed in the Korean way of life and deepening my appreciation of Confucius. I had also encountered the other major influences in people's lives such as Buddhism and Shamanism, so the next challenge would be to get to know them better.

When I left Hwa Yan Ni there were over 2,500 people in the parish community and I knew every one of them by name, their family connections and where they lived. We met regularly on Sundays and at the *huis*. We had annual picnics, sports days, pilgrimages and other celebrations.

Seven years later I returned to Hwa Yang Ni just as the weekday Mass was ending. There was a Korean priest in charge and Bundo was gone. Among the people I met coming out of the church there was only one who knew me. Maybe I would have met more if I had gone on a Sunday but in Seoul the majority of people do not own their home and move on an average every three years. The old house was gone, a new church had been built but the bell tower still stood seven stories tall.

Chapter 5
Civic Riots and Unruly Spirits

After a holiday in Ireland I returned in September 1975 to take over the parish of Haeng Dang Dong, in the same areas as Hwa Yang Ni but closer to the city centre.

My plans extended no further than continuing on the lines I had started in my first parish but the situation in Korea had changed and the atmosphere was different.

The Haeng Dang hill had been occupied by squatters after the Korean War. By the time I got there the shacks on one side had been levelled and public housing apartments, 25 storeys high, raised in their place. A quarry was dug out of the other side of the hill, leaving a flat shelf in the slope, occupied by our church. It was an unusual site with a sheer wall of granite at the back and the front looking out over Seoul's southern suburbs.

I would be the third pastor there. Five years previously the first man had built a single-storey, rectangular building with money he got from the Columbans. There were plans to add another floor when funds were available and in the meantime most of the lower floor was used as a church with the remainder partitioned off as the priest's residence. It was known locally as the 'quarry church.'

The first few months in a new parish can be very lonely. It takes time to get to know the people, and for them to get to know you, but the basic parish structure was familiar with district leaders, parish council and a number of *huis*.

Korea had taken another step forward. Living standards were improving and the county took pride in its modern motorways, shipyards and conglomerates that would shortly become international brands: Gold Star, Samsung, Hyundae, Kia and Daewoo. Two unplanned consequences were the beginning of a passionate struggle for more democracy that would continue for another twenty years and a tug-of-war between the traditional world view and modern Western thinking that would last even longer.

President Park Chung Hee had made the economic growth possible with his Five Year Plans, emphasising infrastructure and moving from light industry to heavy but to achieve this he needed dictatorial powers. It was easier to level houses for new streets and run highways through farm land when no one dared object. Such leadership was tolerable in the early stages of recovery but the people came to resent it as the degree of political freedom failed to match the new prosperity.

In 1972, while I was still in Hwa Yang Ni, the President issued a decree prohibiting criticism of his regime and the new *Yushin* Constitution which cemented his control. His justification was that the country was under constant threat of attack from the North. This message was reinforced by ordering all new houses to have a bomb-proof basement and compelling everyone to join in regular air-raid practices. When the sirens went off you had to stop what you were doing and run to the nearest shelter. There was already a curfew from midnight to 5.00 am. He hoped these reminders of the threat from the North would silence the demand for labour unions, the right of all citizens to participate in electing the president and freedom of the press.

An unexpected anti-government icon appeared in the form of Bishop Daniel Tji of Wonju, a diocese that had been broken off from the northern Columban diocese of Chunchon. While leadership was now in the hands of local clergy, Columbans still staffed half of the parishes and strongly supported the bishop.

In 1970 Bishop Tji had co-founded the Munwha Broadcasting Company in Wonju. This radio station was not particularly political at the time but his involvement in broadcasting opened Bishop Tji's eyes to the corruption in society. He began to complain about the restrictions on the media and in 1974 was arrested and sentenced to 15 years in jail for 'giving financial support to student reformers.'

This led the Korean Bishops, who until then had kept out of politics, to issue a statement entitled, 'Fighting for Justice is the Duty of Bishops.' The Catholic Church was soon the only institution left which was willing to speak out and began to take the lead in the struggle for justice and human rights.

1975 was a 'Holy Year' for Catholics and to inaugurate it in Korea a celebration was held in the national seminary at Hae-Hwa Dong, Seoul. Over a hundred priests participated, both Korean and foreign, and after the Mass, instead of heading back to the sacristy to unvest, the Korean priest at the head of the procession led us down the driveway and out onto the street. As soon as the twelve or so bishops leading the procession emerged from the seminary gate, riot police surrounded them and hustled them to the far side of the road.

For the next two hours there was a stand-off. The bishops in their robes and mitres on one side of the usually busy thoroughfare, ringed in by riot police, and we priests and seminarians in white albs massed at the seminary gate opposite them. Signs with 'Release Bishop Tji' soon appeared.

As traffic on the main street was blocked, an agreement was finally reached and the bishops allowed to return to the seminary. We went back up the hill to unvest but I was worried about the high school students I had promised to meet at the gate after the Mass. Some had come from Hwa Yang Ni and others from my new parish.

When I ventured out to the main road again, floods of protestors were moving past, preparing to march downtown. Some of them shouted at me, 'Come and join us. They won't attack a foreign priest.' I was not too sure about that but as I had to go in their direction to meet the students I went along. They put me on the side where I was clearly visible.

Before we got to Hae-Hwa crossroads the riot police formed ranks to prevent us going any further. Then they charged us, spread in a line across the road, shouting and waving their batons. There was no turning back. As the police came closer, they broke through the front lines of protestors. Soon it was a matter of survival and demonstrators scattered in all directions, some falling as they were hit.

Suddenly l was in the front line and saw a policemen coming at me with a raised baton. All I could do was raise my arms to protect myself and try to look at his eyes through the metal grid over his face. He was an older man and I could see the surprise when he recognised a foreigner. He brushed me aside with his arm and a grunt that probably meant, 'Get out of here.' Unexpectedly I found myself in the area behind, quiet now that the police had passed on.

Fortunately my student friends had avoided the worst of the riot and when we got together we went to a nearby eating-house to discuss our adventures and recover.

The demonstrations were to be a regular occurrence for the next twenty years in one form or another. It was a period in which young Koreans struggled to express, often violently, their hopes for a more just and democratic Korea in which prosperity would be shared. We were involved to different degrees, depending on our situations, but in the 1970s Bishop Tji's imprisonment was of special concern to the Columbans in his northern diocese of Wonju.

During social gatherings at the Columban central house on a Monday night the tension could be felt. The men from the country parishes would imply that those in the city did not show enough commitment to Bishop Tji's cause. Often they would have attended two or three 'prayer meetings' a week in different country parishes but did not see many Columbans from Seoul present. The police could not prevent 'prayer meetings' in church yards so they had become the visible places for dissent.

The Seoul men would reply that they could not participate in all the gatherings outside the city because they were alone in busy, growing parishes.

I could sympathise with them as Haeng Dang Dong did absorb a lot of energy. Because of the inflow of newcomers, spurred by the Church's stand for social justice, we were drawing up plans for a new church on the upper floor. Following the example of Hwa Yang Ni, rather than employing a construction company, we got a local expert to supervise the building and the parish council bought the materials at the cheapest price they could find.

While interest in Christianity, and especially the Catholic Church, grew rapidly among students and intellectuals in the '70s due to the stand of Bishop Tji and Cardinal Stephen Kim, the concerns of the majority of Haeng Dang Dong people were more basic.

Confucianism may be the outward face of Asia but at the heart of everyday life in Korea, and other large areas of Asia, is Shamanism. I had first come across it in Jeju but found it throbbing in the background wherever I went. On our lofty perch in Haeng Dang Dong hardly a day went past without hearing the clash of cymbals and drums announcing a *kut* or séance in progress somewhere below.

When studying in Ottawa I came across Mircea Eliade's acclaimed *Shamanism* and read it from cover to cover. Eliade was born in Romania and became professor of History of Religions in Chicago. His interest in the topic came from his Romanian roots as the Shamanistic influence can be found all over northern Europe, Siberia, the Americas and north-east Asia. It re-entered Western consciousness when Carlos Castaneda wrote his books on the *Teachings of Don Juan* in 1972.

If a religion is seen as a fixed set of beliefs and practices then Shamanism must be the earliest and most widespread of world religions. Its main concern is with the spirit world, to discover the cause of illness and bad fortune. A Shaman, in Korea usually a woman, goes into a trance with the help of dance or drink and ascends by means of a symbolic tree to the upper world where she meets the spirits and finds out why they are displeased with the people back on earth. Then she returns to let her clients know how they can be cured or have good luck restored.

Korean Shamans use music and dance as an entry to trance and an atmosphere is created with colourful flags and dress, drum beat and rice wine. In rural areas there were annual or bi-annual *kuts* for the welfare of the village that could last a week, while in the cities *kuts* at funerals or times of misfortune lasted two or three days.

The topic of unhelpful spirits came up regularly at our monthly house meetings in Haeng Dang Dong.

At one gathering in the public housing apartments beside us, Grandmother Kwon spoke up. A quiet elderly lady, I knew her as a stalwart of the Funeral Society and faithful attender at all church activities.

We were discussing un-earthly beings and miracle cures when she matter-of-factly mentioned that she had been an assistant *mudang* or Shaman. Her role was that of pole-holder. When the *mudang* began a séance to expel a spirit or discover the reason for some misfortune, she held a pole upright in the middle of the arena. Then the *mudang* sang, danced and beat a drum until she reached a state of ecstasy and the familiar spirit came upon her. When she returned to her normal self she revealed the knowledge she had discovered.

Often the *mudang*'s questions were addressed to the pole held by an assistant like Grandmother Kwon and if it moved the answer was 'yes' but if it remained still, the answer was 'no.' When an evildoer or the responsible person is to be located, the pole swayed in his or her direction and might even hit them.

The pole is said to move by its own power and not that of the person holding it.

This fascinated us. One of the ladies asked Grandmother Kwon, 'Did the stick really move of its own accord?'

She answered vehemently, 'I should know it did. How could I tell what answer to give or what I was supposed to do? After a session my arms and sides were so sore I thought I would die.' She was convinced the *mudangs* had real power.

Her explanation was that, as a Christian, the God she believed in was supreme but there were other powers which are subject to him. They often fought among themselves and bothered people. *Mudangs* are involved in modifying these activities but their power does not come from God, at least not directly.

A woman living down near the main road told a similar story. She was sick for a number of years and then discovered that she had psychic powers. Everyone agreed that 'a spirit had come upon her.' When her daughter returned after a long absence the mother could tell her where she had been, describing every detail of the houses she had visited. At times like that, when she talked of spiritual experiences, her voice became that of a man, indicating that the spirit that had come upon her was not her own.

Her neighbours told her she should become a *mudang* but the family were against it. It was not a reputable occupation.

One day the daughter brought a visitor home and the mother said, 'I know where you are from, you are from the Catholic Church. My spirit told me to join the church since my family won't tolerate my spirit contact. I cannot just send him out immediately, seeing he has been with me for a long time. Come back in a few days and I will talk with you.'

No one had known who the visitor was and that she had come to suggest the woman should come to the church.

I found it interesting that people who had given up their *mudang* practices and joined the church still maintained belief in the reality of the spiritual powers they had experienced. Catholics were expected to avoid Shamans because of the superstition involved and to rely on the Church for blessings and exorcisms. However, even those who had given up Shamanism still respected its powers.

During my first Holy Week in Haeng Dang Dong, I was preparing for the Easter Vigil liturgy when three of our most zealous volunteers brought a patient to me. They said she was possessed by a devil and wanted me to cure her. Before we were ordained as priests we had been given the 'Order' of exorcist but I never thought I would be called to exercise it. It was my test case.

The 'possessed' lady did not seem to be particularly abnormal. She appeared to be in a daze but her companions assured me she could get very violent and she had definitely been taken over by an evil spirit. I brought them into the church, found the book of exorcisms, put on a surplice and armed myself with a supply of holy water.

I read the impressive Latin formulas in the book and added a few Korean prayers to keep them in touch with what I was saying and then sprinkled the lady with the water. Nothing outward happened except she seemed to get even quieter. However her companions were satisfied and said they would bring her back in the evening for the Easter ceremonies. She was not a Catholic but they believed that time spent in the church would help her. I was relieved to have escaped so lightly.

Easter is a busy time in a parish so I had asked a fellow Columban, Liam McCarron, to come and help that night. A large crowd of people arrived early and we were kept occupied. When it was time for the ceremonies to begin I went to the sacristy to prepare and Liam continued with the confessions.

The liturgy began at the back of the church where the Easter candle was lit and then we processed up the middle of the church singing, 'This is the Light of Christ.' I was halfway up the aisle when a loud screeching began that drowned out the choir. The sound was coming from the lady who had been 'cured' that morning. Her three companions were with her, trying to quieten her. I wondered if the 'Light of Christ' had disturbed her demon.

I also observed Liam coming out of the confessional looking rather startled. He was just back from a course in Clinical Pastoral Education in Boston and was about to start a counselling service. I hoped that the encounter between evil spirits and the new techniques of psychiatry would be an enlightening occasion for him. After a few minutes the noise stopped and we were able to continue with the ceremony. Afterwards when we were recovering Liam refused to give me his impression of the lady based on his recent studies. However it was not the last time I was to be involved with evil spirits.

A few months later, two district leaders asked me to come with them to the house of a girl who was possessed. The family were not Catholic and they had just held a *kut* to no avail. Now they wanted me to do what I could. I followed them to the house, took off my shoes at the doorway and climbed through the raised door into the room which was already packed with relatives.

Trying to communicate with the girl, who was in her early twenties, was difficult with family members listening to every word. Recalling some of the advice given for such situations, I looked for evidence that an evil spirit was involved but could not find any. Rather there seemed to be a dispute about marriage plans.

As on the previous occasion I said the prayers and sprinkled water and while it did not seem to me to have any effect one way or the other, the family thought they saw an improvement. Maybe they believed the foreign Shaman should be more effective than the local version. The girl became quieter too. I talked with her for a while, trying to reassure her, and she seemed to appreciate what I was saying. I asked her to come to the church to see me when she felt better and she nodded.

Before I left I suggested to the family that they bring the girl to a doctor as she might need medical care. They said they would think about it. I did not want to mention the words 'mental problem' as that would have been as offensive as saying she had leprosy but I added that I did not think she was possessed by a spirit.

Two days later I met one of the district leaders who had brought me to the house and asked how the girl was.

'Oh,' she said. 'Did you not hear? She died yesterday.'

'How?' I asked, shaken.

'She committed suicide,' she replied.

I wondered if there was anything else I could have done.

As it happened, shortly afterwards an American priest, Fr Francis McNutt, came to Seoul to give talks and retreats on the Charismatic Movement. One of the popular books he had written was *Deliverance from Evil Spirits* so I signed up for his three-day course. Perhaps unfortunately for him, fifteen other Columbans did also and it would be hard to find a tougher audience.

Nothing seemed to faze Francis however and he impressed me by saying after the first lecture that there would be no more talking, we would immediately get down to the practical business of faith healing and casting out devils.

We began with healing sessions for those among the participants who had medical problems and met with mixed success. Then we moved to the downtown cathedral and people were invited to come forward to be cured. The church was packed. Two by two we were told where to stand and people were asked to come to us for healing prayers. On my way to our assigned place I came across a group of my parishioners with a lady who had been confined to her apartment for the past three years. She was not a Catholic when she moved in but she could see our church from her window and got some of her neighbours to come and instruct her in the faith.

When we thought she was sufficiently prepared, I baptised her in her room and regularly brought her the sacraments. Now here she was in person, miles from home. Fortunately she and her companions were on their way to where Fr McNutt was standing and I was not called on to help her further.

During the service there were occasional periods of loud screaming, mainly from the area where Fr McNutt was positioned. The combined efforts of my companion and myself did not have any dramatic effects though the people seemed to be satisfied to be prayed over.

Later I asked the ladies I had met in the cathedral how our friend had fared. They said that she had not been cured but she was very happy with the outing and being blessed by Fr McNutt himself. His prayers might not have brought the desired result for her but the ladies claimed he had cured a man with paralysed legs and a woman with a throat complaint.

The Charismatic Movement became quite popular for a while and then settled down in most parishes with a loyal group of followers. It seemed to be one of the few occasions when the Church did respond positively to popular religiosity. While I never became an enthusiast myself, it raised my awareness of the Spirit moving in the world around me and in other people. In a Church which had taught that the Spirit worked principally through the Pope, bishops and other superiors it was refreshing to be reminded that the original gospel message emphasised that the Spirit moved in all and could be found in the most unexpected places.

Encounters with *mudangs* and spirits in Haeng Dang Dong made me more respectful of the people's awareness of 'another world' and how it interacts with this world. Later, living closer to the people in Shillim-Dong, I had others opportunities to see what the spirits meant to ordinary people but I was never sure how to respond. As a Christian I believed in one God, and a compassionate God at that, but did that exclude the existence of other non-human beings? It also seemed too much to expect people who for most of their lives were conscious of the presence of spirits to abandon those beliefs immediately and completely.

This question was very much on my mind when my life in Haeng Dang Dong was interrupted by an unexpected event. I was elected as a delegate from Korea to our General Chapter of 1976, to be held in the Philippines. Since it was my first time to attend a General Chapter, I looked forward to meeting the men working in other parts of Asia and Latin America and hearing how they were dealing with the challenges of popular religion, evil spirits and deep cultural differences.

In fact the Chapter delegates had other issues on their minds and it was those immediate realities which would dominate discussions.

Chapter 6
Delegate from Korea

The Chapter was held in Baguio, the Philippines, from 4 October to 8 December 1976 with forty-five members representing the twelve different countries in which Columbans worked.

The Philippines is just a four-hour flight south from Seoul, passing over Jeju on the way, but those four hours were significant. Manila was hot, tropical green and rich with exotic fruits. There was papaya and a squeeze of calamansi for breakfast and mangoes for snacks during the day. Low cool buildings and an unhurried atmosphere were a change from the bustle of commerce and construction in Seoul which was then slipping into its icy winter. The economic and religious differences were just as striking.

Up to the 1960s the Philippines had been one of the richest countries in Asia, now it was among the poor. It was hard to understand why that happened as the people are well educated and talented, and there are plenty of natural resources. Families make great sacrifices to send one or two of their children to university and English is widely spoken, especially in the northern island of Luzon. It is the only Catholic nation in Asia, dating from the mid-1500s. Yet for some reason it seemed unable to make the most of its human and natural potential.

According to our men who worked there, conservative *haciendero* families in the provinces controlled politics and big business and had no interest in a more democratic system. The country was also a federation of islands with different languages and cultures so the sense of belonging to one nation was weak. Under Ferdinand Marcos the county had been united and prospered for a period but, as happened in Korea, the innovator become a dictator and the old disunity re-emerged.

We did not spend long in Manila but were bussed up the mountains to Baguio where the Chapter would be held. Traffic congestion in the capital was so bad that we had to leave at 4.30 am before gridlock set in.

Because of the moderate climate that comes with an altitude of 1,540 metres, Baugio is a refreshing contrast to the constant heat below. In 1903 it was designated 'Summer Capital of the Philippines' by the Americans who occupied the country and every summer the administration would transfer its operations there to escape the heat of Manila. The name itself, given by the local Ibaloi people, meant 'moss' and once outside the town there was the fresh clean scent of a cool pine forest.

It was not just the Americans who appreciated the lower temperatures of Baguio, many religious groups had residences there for educational purposes or just giving their members a break from the energy-sapping heat. The house we met in was called 'Sunnyside' but it was surrounded by pine trees which did not let much sunlight in. It also rained for an hour every afternoon and we from the cooler north would not have objected to a little more of the tropical heat.

Chapters were gatherings at which serious decisions guiding the future of the Society were supposed to be made. However two issues were to dominate the discussions and create tension during the two-month event.

One was a dispute that had arisen among the members of the Society's central leadership. Vatican II had led to expectation of greater openness and from 1968 young people in the Western world had begun to express their frustrations forcefully. It was inevitable that a group like ours could not escape unscathed.

A student had been dismissed from the seminary in Dalgan and a member of the Central Council, which advises the Superior General, felt the student had not been treated justly. The issue was debated to exhaustion by the Council members themselves and the majority decided that the incident had been dealt with properly, in accordance with church law, and there was no basis for complaint.

However, the champion of the dismissed student claimed that the student's human rights were being ignored and brought the matter to the attention of others, including the national press. Suddenly the Irish papers were devoting whole pages to the case and writing editorials about it. After a number of efforts towards mediation it was decided to bring the dispute to the next General Chapter.

Months had gone into preparing an elaborate consultative process on recent changes in the church and the world but, once the representatives gathered, those plans had to abandoned and time given to the disagreement. I was one of a three man sub-committee appointed to review all the related documents and summarise them in a report with recommendations. Our findings were discussed and then handed over to another sub-committee who came up with an even shorter and vaguer statement which was accepted but left no one completely satisfied. The Superior General, who felt responsibility for what happened, was publicly vindicated but would not put his name forward for re-election.

This debate took up much of the Chapter's time and energy and, although it led to clearer guidelines for dealing with future disputes, it reduced time that should have been devoted to the second major topic, the 'Aim and Nature' of the Society. The extent to which mission and its message had radically changed was taken up at the previous Chapter, in 1970, and serious differences emerged which were too complex to be dealt with fully at that time.

I was not surprised that this issue was at the top of list and it echoed the question which had stayed with me since my encounter in Kangjin. If 'saving souls' was no longer urgent, what should missionaries be doing?

Many of the older men thought that we should just continue to build up parishes and take care of local communities. Younger men insisted that we needed to be more involved with the poor and those treated unjustly in society, even if it meant distancing ourselves from church structures. For them, the Kingdom should be expressed more in social and economic terms.

I could sympathise with both but felt there was a deeper question which I was slow to bring up in formal discussions both in deference to the greater experience of other delegates and my own difficulty in pinpointing it.

How could we work effectively either with parish communities or among those deprived of basic rights if we were not familiar with their background, thinking and values? We had never been trained to immerse ourselves in another civilisation and appreciate the people's own deepest concerns. We still didn't see any urgency in making up for our earlier lack of preparation for that task.

The effect this had on our work was becoming more and more obvious, to me at least. At the same time I could understand, if not accept, the main reasons for this lack of interest in other cultures.

It was taken for granted that the church would be much the same all around the world. When we arrived in Korea Mass was still celebrated in Latin and so were all the important liturgies. This meant that we could be involved in church activities immediately without too much emphasis on language skills. Preaching did demand some knowledge of the local language but we only needed to repeat Church teaching and practices, the message was the same always and everywhere.

No one thought it strange that the standard seven-year course for diocesan priests in the English speaking world was sufficient for missionaries going to Asia, Africa or South America, with only minor changes.

If we had any distinctive mission-related studies, it was a choice between Spanish and French. At that time the Pope was stressing the needs in Latin America so many of us opted for Spanish. That was in our second and third years and by the time we finished our seventh year we had forgotten most of it. As it turned out, that didn't matter because when our class of twenty newly ordained got our appointments, we found we were going to the Philippines, Korea, Japan and Burma. No one was sent to Latin America and only the Philippines used a little Spanish.

We arrived in Korea with no prior knowledge of its language, culture and history. We knew there had been a war there recently, there was now a truce and the country was divided North and South. However, our lack of preparation did not worry us. We were part of an international organisation whose members had wide experience in our assigned country and we would just have to follow the example of those before us.

As I had learnt in Jeju, church structures in Korea were little different from those in Ireland. The priest was in complete control and had a catechist who acted as intermediary with the local authorities, got jobs done around the compound, instructed newcomers to the Church and even told the people after the priest's sermon, 'Now this is what Father really meant to say.'

We would be in the country for six years before going home on vacation for the first time so we tackled the language conscientiously and, fortunately, without pressure. Our first six months of Korean studies were at our central house in Seoul and taught by a young man who was doing his Masters at a university, Seo Chong-su. Later he was to be of great help to as president of the parish council in Hwa Yang Ni. He had designed his own text book and patiently pushed us into speaking like Koreans. Then, after two years 'out in the field' (Jeju for me), we returned for another six months course at Yon-sae University.

The language classes were the best available at the time and we realised they were just the beginning. The US Army Language School in Hawaii considered Korean the hardest language to learn because, among other things, its sentences do not follow the subject-verb-object order with which Westerners were familiar. This is why our teacher had to 'patiently push us into speaking the Korean way.' We learnt patterns rather than words and changed the wording of the pattern to suit the situation.

If you wanted to ask, 'Which is the road to Seoul?' you said, 'To Seoul going road where is it?' using the correct speech level, depending on whom you are addressing. You just changed the name of the town or object in the pattern as the occasion demanded.

While a lot of attention was given to language studies after 1960, there was little emphasis on the culture and history of the country. It did not matter that the people had three thousand year-old traditions, they were seen as outdated.

Nor did the state of the country in the 1960s and early 70s encourage efforts to understand and respect the ways of the people.

The Korean War had ended just ten years before we arrived but in our eyes it could have been six months. There were few large buildings left in Seoul, rows of single storey shops and houses lined muddy lanes. The only articles on sale were basic foods and second-hand clothing. Vehicles on the road were military, either American or ROK (Republic of Korea) jeeps. The majority of people were impoverished. American relief agencies were still distributing grain and milk powder through on-the-ground organisations like the Columbans. Demands to understand Korean culture and history were not pressing.

Amid so much devastation and poverty, modern Western education and methods seemed the obvious way to a better future and, since Western civilization was based on Christian values and attitudes, we saw Christianity and progress as going hand in hand.

Our contacts with the US Army reinforced our belief that the future was with the new, bright Western model. There were two American infantry divisions in Korea at the time, the 1st and the 7th Infantry, with over 10,000 men each plus various supporting services so the total came to about 50,000. The combat divisions were stationed along the DMZ (De-Militarised Zone) as the first line of defence against North Korean attacks. As it happened, one of the two dioceses staffed by Columbans stretched along that border. With Western missionaries and Americans GIs isolated together in mountainous terrain and facing similar difficulties, there was bound to be interaction.

The headquarters of Eight Army, which controlled all military activity in South Korea, was in Yongsan in Seoul and we had regular contact with army chaplains on their way from, or back to, the front line.

Since the U.S. soldiers were on a 13-month tour of duty they had no incentive to learn the language or show respect for local culture. They were confined to barbwire-enclosed camps and all they knew of the local populace was through the Ville, and that was not likely to give a positive impression. Conversations with them usually brought up the latest stories about 'slickly boy' thieves and how personal belongings, jeeps and even camp bulldozers disappeared mysteriously.

We felt close to the American military in our early years in Seoul. Having Mass at the camps on Sundays was a welcomed break from language studies. It introduced us to 'Little America' with its shiny PX supermarkets, cinemas, bowling alleys, golfclub and steak restaurants.

On the weekend we would be driven up to Camp Casey or Red Cloud in a staff car, redeployed to outlying chapels and maybe taken to lunch or the PX afterward by the chaplain. It was hard to resist the lure of America with its luxuries, informality and success. We shared its sense of humour, sports and priorities.

One Sunday I was at the back of the chapel in Uijeongbu (pronounced 'Wee-John-boo' by the GIs) when a new chaplain introduced himself to the troops during Mass.

'My name is John Chmieleweski,' he said, 'C-H-M-I-E-L-E-W-E-S-K-I. It's a Polish name so my brother cut it down to "C-H-E-M-I-S-K-I". However I stuck with the original spelling and when I went to a school run by Brothers, the teacher asked me my name. When I told him, he said, "Too hard, we'll call you Murphy." Then a Murphy came to the school and he said, "We'll call you Ryan". Then a Ryan came and he said, "OK, We'll settle for "You, there." The soldiers loved it.

While the American military were most generous to us, and provided the few western luxuries we enjoyed, they were not the best company to keep if you wanted to learn about Korean culture.

There was also a negative attitude towards local religions coming from our Church background. On one occasion in those early days, I mentioned to our boss in Seoul that I was beginning to see something familiar and attractive in Korean beliefs. He immediately showed concern. 'A lot of it is superstition and from the devil,' he warned me in all seriousness. His attitude was shared by many of the older priests who had been brought up in a rather black-and-white world view.

The first Columbans came to the country in 1933 when the 'Ancestral Rites' ban was still in force and many gave the impression that, as far as they were concerned, the prohibitions remained.

Another factor was the rural isolation within which Columbans worked. Our eighty or so men in Korea at that time lived in small country towns or villages along the northern DMZ or in the rural Cholla province. They were lucky if they got together once a week.

Long rains at the beginning of summer could lead to serious flooding and further limited communication. During one such downpour the newly appointed bishop of the northern Wonju diocese, Daniel Tji, drove out to see how an isolated Columban was getting on. He got as far as a flooded river and found that the low hill on which the church was built had become a mid-stream island. The priest seemed determined to stay there with his people till the waters subsided so the bishop called over to him, 'Father, you are a saint.' The priest is said to have called back, 'Bishop, I am a .... idiot!'

In the same rugged area two Columbans were returning home late at night went their jeep broke down. They didn't even have a torch so could not investigate what was wrong. However there was a light in the distance and they set out to get help. When they got to the house one called out in Korean, 'Anyone there?' and eventually a man emerged cautiously with a lamp. The priest asked, 'Could you lend me a candle *(chaw)*?' The man looked offended and said something sharp in return. The priest repeated his request and the man got even more excited. The second priest interrupted, 'Be careful, Mike,' he said. 'I think you are asking him for a loan of his wife.' The word for wife was *chaw* and for candle *cho*.

That sense of humour and awareness of their own shortcomings kept the missionaries rooted in reality. When they gathered in Seoul or their local central house they got an evening's entertainment sharing such stories.

Isolation meant the priests had little encouragement or opportunity to explore local traditions. Due to the lack of proper language schools up to the 1960s, many of them were not fluent in Korean and much of what they did know was 'church talk' which could be incomprehensible to non-Catholics. Few ever met non-Catholics as equals or had a chance to learn from them.

News of the wider world was limited too. In Seoul there were two English-language newspapers which were carefully censored. Local papers were in Korean and used Chinese characters which made them almost impossible to read. While some men had short-wave radios that got the BBC in the middle of the night (for news and the rugby internationals), most relied on the American Forces Radio (AFKN) and the army newspaper, *Stars and Stripes*. As a result many Columbans in Korea became well informed on American football, basketball and ice hockey.

I could sympathise with some of the reasons why we were so slow to take Korean culture and religions seriously and guessed that in other countries in which we worked the attitude was similar, even if circumstances differed slightly. However as professional missionaries we should have been pioneers in Korean studies.

Few of the other delegates showed the same concerns and there was no space for the topic on the Baguio Chapter agenda. Changes were on their way but the interest of our members had more to do with the tension between parish work and 'special ministries' than digging deeper into local religions. We were trained for parish ministry and were slow to encourage members to get involved with workers, youth, the handicapped or Alcohol Anonymous outside familiar structures.

In the Chapter's final statement the task of bringing the Gospel alive in cultures not our own was mentioned along with that of seeking the full Christian liberation of the poor and oppressed. This seemed to satisfy everyone but the men in Latin America would continue to see 'dialogue with other religions' differently from those working in Asia, and the members in Korea and Japan would continue to look on 'full Christian liberation for the poor and oppressed' with less urgency than those in Chile and Peru.

There was also a last-minute list of practical proposals: to set up a commission for the Chinese Apostolate, to find a place for laity in mission and to increase the commitment to Latin America. Taking a stance for human rights might lead to confrontation with civil authorities so it directed that guidelines be drawn up to deal with that possibility including a contingency plan in case all the members were expelled from a country.

The ideas were good and it would take years for them to be fully appreciated and implemented. Yet, I felt we had missed an opportunity. In the parishes I knew in Korea, people both well-off and poor were looking for something more than an institutional church and progressive social movements. Whether they were upright Confucianists, retired shamans like Grandmother Kwon, occasional Temple supplicants or clients of fortune tellers their search was for something deeper on which to base their lives. We could have spent more time finding out what was being done about that in each country and drawing up concrete measures to improve the situation but there was little enthusiasm for the task at the Chapter.

On returning to Korea I was happy to continue where I had left off, not unduly worried that attitudes would be slow to change. There was enough challenge in Haeng Dang Dong. Our community kept growing and I was still intrigued by the mischievous spirits and faith healing. My thoughts on local life continued to appear in *The Korea Times*. However the need to do more about cultural issues kept nagging at me and once again I was fortunate. Early in 1978 I was asked to return to Ireland as Communications Officer for the Irish Missionary Union with the task of telling people about the new activities in which missionaries were getting involved. It was an opportunity to see what was to be learnt from Africa and Latin America.

Yet, leaving Haeng Dang Dong was not a simple matter. There was another emotional farewell party and it made me realise how close we had become as a community during those two-and-a-half years. Only a few months previously we had celebrated my feast day, St Hugo's on 17 November, and afterward I had been presented with a photo album record of the event. It was a happier occasion than a departure ceremony, though following a remarkably similar format, and as I still have the album I can relive that afternoon, the people, their generosity and how they expressed themselves.

With a Confucian sense of order, the album saw the occasion as divided into three steps: 'Part 1, Celebration of Mass; Part 2, Presentation of Gifts; Part 3, Congratulatory Meal.'

Part 1 was represented by fourteen photos with sub-titles. There was, 'Fr Min (my Korean name) giving the homily' and 'Paul Yun Reading the Epistle.' Paul was vice-chairman of the Parish Council. His brother was a well-known doctor who had founded the Catholic hospital in the city centre, but Paul lived modestly with his family in Haeng Dang Dong, running a small factory producing medical instruments. Other photos showed the choir, mostly women, six altar servers with red 'beanies' on their heads, and shots of the congregation from small children to grandparents. The Mass was celebrated in our new 'upper floor' church built with the people's own money and free from debt within a year.

Part 2 showed me, 'Listening to the Congratulatory Speech of the Chairman, Raphael Lim.' Raphael was a quiet man who showed it was possible to be a *kunja* and businessman at the same time. He owned a garage at the bottom of the hill and had got me a second hand Kia car for next to nothing and kept it running for me. I did not need a car in a parish which had few lanes wide enough to accommodate it but it was useful to visit other parishes and bring people to meetings.

The next pages of the album showed, 'Fr Min Gives His Response.' This speech was also a formality but after using the initial required polite phrases I was able to lapse into less honorific language as I listed some of our happier memories. This was followed by a presentation of flowers by two little girls in traditional dress and a gift from the people of the parish presented by Peter Cheong, a retired tradesman who was ready to do anything from performing as emergency best man to de-freezer when the water pipes were frozen solid.

Peter Oh brought a gift from the Joseph Society. Peter ran a building supplies shop on the main road and knew all the men in the area mainly through drinking sessions with them. Despite his partying habits he prided himself on his strength and physique. The members of the Joseph's Society were mainly couples in his neighbourhood and I had attended many of their lively celebrations.

Beata Kim came up, representing the Funeral Society, and Lucy Pak of the Vincent De Paul Society brought more gifts.

The Stephen Society, for newly-baptised adults, was represented by John Kim, a local post office official, and he was followed by a representative of the Junior Legion and children from the Sunday School. By then the area around the altar was a mound of presents.

After a round of satisfied clapping, everyone moved downstairs for the party.

The first photo in Part Three was captioned 'Fr Min sits in the place of honour,' and indeed he looked contented. Then there are shots of the people seated at tables eating spicy Korean dishes and drinking soft drinks or beer. Finally the entertainment began. Children performed dances they had learnt in kindergarten, the Young Christian Workers (Haeng Dang branch), dressed in colourful traditional dress, sang and a high school girl played a traditional *ky-ya-gum*. I did not recognise her so she must have been brought in specially to add to the occasion.

There were folk songs from high schoolgirls in traditional dress, captioned 'demure,' though four other girls in school uniform were labelled '*wol-ga-dak*' which means cheeky. Even among the adults these three young ladies were known for their outgoing cheerfulness and their confidence that, with safety in numbers, they could say anything they wanted to me and get what they requested.

Then the adults took over the singing and dancing, 'Without getting tired,' as the caption noted. All the familiar faces were there and, no surprise, Peter Oh standing on his hands on the stage edge. When wine is consumed, Confucian standards are put aside.

In March when I was about to leave, the celebration was on similar lines though this time with more crying than laughing. You couldn't find a more heart-rending event than a Children's Mass at which a little girl comes forward to read a farewell letter spelling out how much you will be missed and breaks down sobbing in the middle of it. A teacher takes it up and completes reading the letter with tears in her eyes and a choking voice. Who said Orientals are unemotional?

Hwa Yang Ni had been unique, it was my first parish and the one in which 1 was longest, but Haeng Dang Dong was special too and I still hear from my friends there.

Chapter 7
Bringing Back the Message

On my journey back to Ireland I had another chance to visit parts of India and Africa. It helped to say I was doing it to prepare for my work with the IMU.

Bombay (now Mumbai) was the first stop as I wanted to visit the Liturgical Centre in Bangalore run by Fr D S Amalorpavadass, a controversial figure trying to integrate the Catholic Church into Indian religious traditions. The Indian Church was proud that it had been founded by the apostle Thomas and the early Catholics had no qualms about including local customs and practices into their Christian marriages and funerals. Their processions involved dance, flowers and fire, their churches resembled temples and their ways of worship began with the *anjali hasta,* bowing deeply with hands joined on the forehead. Drawing from the symbol-rich Indian heritage came naturally to them.

However the Western missionaries who arrived in the 16th century compelled them to change to the Roman rite with it foreign practices. After Vatican II, scholars like Fr Amalorpavadass began testing the new freedoms to explore and adapt. He set up his Bangalore research centre in Indian temple style and lived there as a traditional Indian teacher.

The day I visited was a quiet one, there were no students around and l would not be able to witness a Mass celebrated in the new manner. However I met Fr Amalorpavadass himself.

In his appearance and attitude he resembled an Indian *guru* or *swami*. Not a tall man, he had a thin intense face and light beard. He wore a white cotton sarong and sat on the floor, isolated in a bright alcove with his back to a sun-lit white colonnade. His spoke quietly and to the point.

I told him of my interest in religious adaptation as I could see the need for it in Korea.

He mentioned that he had been at the Synod of Bishops in Rome in 1974 as an advisor and had encouraged the bishops to include a section on inculturation in their document. His suggestions were not utilised but he got permission to try out an experimental Indian-rite Mass that would eventually replace the imported Latin or Roman liturgy.

Many, including the bishops (his own brother was one), were not enthusiastic about his efforts even though the Vatican had recently come out with a possible '12 Points for Adaptation.' Some South Indian Catholics were so strongly opposed to any form of 'Indianisation' that they took him to court on the grounds that the proposed changes would 'threaten their own distinctive identity.' They were proud to be 'Western' Catholics.

The difficulty lay in distinguishing Indian culture from Hindu religion. Christianity needed a distinct identity, otherwise it would be viewed as a Hindu sect, but it should also be seen as something familiar, emerging out of the people's heritage and not just a foreign intervention. Only then could it challenge aspects of the local culture with its unique message.

While his centre focussed on liturgical adaptation, Fr Amalorpavadass was conscious that there was more to Christianity than ritual and, in a country with serious class and economics divisions, the Church should be involved in seeking equality and justice.

He got up to see me out and gave me copies of some of the articles on inculturation he had written. I left thinking that we still had a long way to go in Korea to produce people like him. Most Korean Catholics, perhaps like the South Indians who opposed Amalorpavadass, admired the Church as a modern Western institution with which they could identify. For now enough of their traditional beliefs found continuity there and even if Christian theological speculation was hard to understand or appreciate, it was a price worth paying to be 'modern.' However I could see that as Korea developed and national pride increased, the people there would also be demanding a more 'Korean' church, reflecting their ancestors' approaches to the sacred.

**

My previous visit to Ethiopia had been in 1969 when I went there to see my sister, Rosaleen, and I had opportunities then to see how Coptic practices added colour to Latin liturgies. The intervening ten years had been traumatic for the people and it was not the same calm and hospitable country I had previously experienced.

The Emperor Haile Selassi had been deposed in September 1974 and the county plunged into chaos as rival Marxist groups fought for control. The most powerful was the Communist Military Junta known as the Derg and when Mengistu Haile Mariam became its leader in 1977 he launched a 'Red Terror' to bring the people into submission. It lasted two years during which 30,000 to 40,000 people died.

When I arrived in Addis Ababa the worst of the 'Red Terror' had passed but unruly groups of revolutionaries still roamed the streets arresting and killing freely. I saw one such mob when taking a stroll around the area where my sister lived but fortunately they were still some distance away and I was able to retreat down a side road. As they passed I reflected that even the streets of Seoul during demonstrations were not as dangerous.

Under the aggressively Marxist government, the Churches were in a precarious position. Many foreign priests and Sisters stayed on and carried out their work quietly in famine areas along with their Ethiopian colleagues but the previously powerful Orthodox Church was under serious pressure.

I was told that an important monastery to the north of the city was interested in meeting a representative of the Irish Church and since I was going to work with the Irish Missionary Union I might qualify. The Orthodox Church had enjoyed many privileges from the royal family and now that the Derg was confiscating their estates they were worried about their future.

With my sister, I drove out to the monastery but when we got there she was not allowed to enter and had to wait in the car while I was went inside the all-male complex.

The institution itself was not one massive building but reminded me of the spread-out Celtic monasteries like Glendalough or even a Buddhist compound. Inside the high walls was a wide open space with a domed church and a few low buildings scattered around.

From the gate a monk in long habit and tall hat led me to a small stone building. It was dark inside as the only widows were on each side of the door through which I had entered. In the middle of the room was a rectangular table and before he left the monk indicated that I should sit at one end of it.

After a short wait in the gloom, the door at the opposite end opened and a tall monk entered. He introduced himself in good English as the Abbot. After inviting me to be seated he rang a bell on the table. Almost immediately doors opened on either side of the room and from each emerged an elderly monk. It seemed the Abbot's council lived in apartments off the meeting room.

The Abbot began by telling me he had heard about the great monastic traditions of Ireland. He wondered if, at this moment of crisis for the Orthodox monasteries in Ethiopia, they would be willing to extend fraternal assistance. Now that their estates were gone, the Ethiopian communities had difficulty in supporting their large number of monks.

To illustrate the problem the Abbot led me back out to the compound. He explained that most of the monks did not live there but alone in the nearby hills. They came together at midday, not for prayer, but to collect their daily meal, a quarter slice of a large circular pancake called *injera* with a portion of beans and vegetables on to it. We watched them as they gathered, lined up for their share and carried it off silently to their hermitages.

I was also shown the church which was large and octagonal but obviously not big enough to hold all the monks if they gathered. It was regarded with such reverence that when Mass was offered people would stand outside the door, feeling unworthy to enter.

The inside itself was divided into three sections, curtained off from each other, with only the priests allowed to enter the final inner sanctum. While standing alone under the dome, waiting for the Abbot who had gone into the inner sanctum, I was startled by an eerie sound coming from above me. Deep and repeated every minute or so, it added to the mysteriousness of the building but I concluded it was doves resting inside the dome. They provided a not unfitting sound effect.

As I left through the tall outer gates, the Abbot repeated his request for assistance. I replied that I would do my best to pass on his message though the Irish monasteries were run by different Religious Orders and were unlikely to respond as a group.

On the way back to Addis I tried to describe for my sister what I had seen and heard. In many ways the Ethiopian Orthodox Church seemed locked in an earlier age with its long liturgies, priestly caste and sacred language. Yet it was part of the people's heritage and was likely to outlast Marxism not only in Ethiopia but in Russia also. It could be seen as a witness to the sanctity of life and nature at a time when both were very much under threat.

**

Back in Ireland in March I went straight to work with the Irish Missionary Union (IMU) which was then located on Wellington Road in Dublin. It had an apartment in the basement into which I moved.

The Union had been set up in 1969 as an umbrella for 60-plus mission sending groups in Ireland. Its services extended from representing missionaries with national organisations, running training courses, doing research, facilitating lay mission, communicating mission activities (my job) as well as office administration and providing travel insurance. There were still over 6000 Irish missionaries abroad but the understanding of mission was changing and concerns for the future were creeping in.

October each year was celebrated as 'Mission Month' and in my first week in the job I was attending meetings on what we would put on the poster to be sent to schools and parishes. All agreed that the old slogan, 'Missionaries save souls,' no longer conveyed the message. We spent hours looking for an alternative. A person going out to spread Christianity needed to know it has something to offer that other religions don't have. What was that element?

At that time there was a growing respect for Oriental religions and it seemed discourteous to suggest that one religion might have more to offer than another. However that question was at the heart of our work at the IMU. Eventually we got around the problem by agreeing on an image of monks setting out in a boat. It had a sense of 'men on a mission,' going out into the unknown, but provided no indication as to what gave urgency to their venture beyond the cross on their sails.

To help clarify what mission was about, both for ourselves and for others, a National Mission Congress at the Marian shrine in Knock was planned for April 1979 with the title 'A Missionary People in the New Missionary Era.' As communications officer my job was to generate interest in the topic and help organise the event. It seemed a good opportunity to show what was happening in different parts of the world and, from concrete examples, to point out how missionaries' understanding of their task had changed.

I began to gather material for a 'coffee table style' book to illustrate the stories of a new generation of Irish missionaries. In the age before faxes, internet and skype information had to be sought, and interviews done, by post. The offer of a free inaugural flight to Arusha in Tanzania also enabled me to get first-hand stories from East Africa.

Arusha, on the eastern edge of the Great Rift Valley, is a centre for sightseeing in the Mt Kilimanjaro region. I was fortunate that my visit to hospitals and rural parishes brought me out into the magnificent countryside and gave me an idea of why people so easily fell in love with Africa.

On one trip we stopped on a low hill looking down into the valley which was over twenty miles wide at that point. Against a background of intense blue sky and green shrub the valley curved gently up to the loft peak of Mt Meru. No animals were visible beneath the bush and the only intrusion in nature was a tiny church, standing alone in the centre with not even a fence around it. An Oriental artist would have savoured the display of nature's immensity, emphasised by the insignificant presence of humans.

In the hospital at Dareda I encountered an aspect of life that was familiar in Korea. During lunch one day there was a discussion on the most common local diseases and their causes. Flies are a major problem but one of the African Sisters who had recently graduated as a doctor said, rather mischievously I thought, 'But of course some of them are due to the devil.'

The other Sisters, mostly European, did not take her comment seriously but I mentioned that I had seen a number of patients said to be possessed by devils in Korea. I was thinking of Haeng Dang Dong. To the people there, the unseen world is not necessarily an unreal world and I recounted some of my experiences.

Maybe the Sister doctor was calling my bluff, but she invited me to join her in a visit to a man in the wards who was possessed by a devil. I declined after short consideration. It was one thing to confront an evil spirit in Korean but to take on an African spirit in a public ward and in his own language seemed too ambitious.

The book that eventually appeared, *Builders of Bridges*, told the stories of twenty-one missionaries who were doing something different. We spent months trying to decide on a title that was both fresh and relevant. Building bridges between cultures and religions seemed a good image though it could give the impression it was an engineering manual.

I already knew a number of those featured in the book, like PJ McGlinchey in Jeju and Sally Fay who had been in Thailand with Viatores Christi lay missionaries and had just returned to Dublin. Thanks to my visit to East Africa I met Richard Walsh in Dar-es-Salaam where he worked as a chaplain in a Socialist University and Brian Hearne in Eldoret, Kenya, where he co-directed the Gaba catechetic centre. In Ethiopia I had got to know Paul Lambert who was seeking ways of collaborating with the Orthodox Church.

In the Philippines I knew the men in Mindinao who were risking their lives along with their community workers in resisting the indiscriminate torture and killing of civil rights activists.

Back in Dublin I was able to interview Bishop Donal Lamont who had recently been expelled from Rhodesia for upholding the rights of black people. To get information for the other stories I depended on postal correspondence. The book was printed in Holland, by the Divine Word Press, and two thousand copies were brought back to Ireland in a returning cattle truck in time for the opening day of the Congress.

I used the photos gathered for the book to make slide shows for a Missionary Exhibition in the main hall and was able to get the different missionary groups to build a 'native hut' to represent each continent and house the audio-visuals.

All the stories illustrated some fresh initiative. In Latin America it was building up faith-based communities in shanty towns. Irish diocesan priests were volunteering to serve in Peru and Chile and it was hoped they would bring back valuable ideas on their return.

In Africa, new catechetical centres were exploring effective ways of sharing the basic Christian message with ordinary people and encouraging liturgies filled with the singing and dancing that came so naturally to them. Yoruba art was being used in church buildings. Missionaries were prepared to leave their compound to follow nomadic peoples. In South Africa and Zimbabwe they were siding with the local black people, setting up night schools to help them improve their prospects. Sisters were moving out of hospitals to establish small clinics and introduce public health schemes in remote villages.

In India and Japan missionaries were living in ashrams and Zen centres as they explored Asian mysticism. William Johnston

SJ had written books on Zen meditation that were helping to popularise Asian spirituality in Ireland.

While my time was devoted to readying the book and the exhibition, the Congress was also encouraging missionaries themselves to reflect on the changing situation. Although I was unable to attend many of the workshops given by international experts the talks were published afterwards by my colleague, Padraig Flanagan, in a book entitled *A New Missionary Era*.

The five-day event created a lot of energy. Busloads of children flocked though the exhibition, picking up every leaflet that caught their eye. Then they moved on to the rock musical with a missionary theme produced by the students of the missionary colleges. The seminars were packed with returned and potential missionaries and those interested in hearing about Church developments since Vatican II.

Latin America captured a lot of attention. Its huge population was nominally Catholic and they were being encouraged to join together in tackling the great poverty and widespread injustice around them. In February, just a few months before the Congress, a major meeting of the Latin American bishops had been held in Puebla, Mexico. An earlier gathering, in Medellin, Colombia, in 1968 had attracted interest when it gave support to the Basic Christian Community movement and the Liberation Theology of Gustavo Gutierrez. It was the first time after Vatican II that bishops had come together on a continental basis and applied the gospel message to their own situation.

The meetings of the Church in Latin America set a new tone by focussing on the basic needs of the people. Bishops urged them to gather in faith communities and have confidence in their own strengths, promising the Church would support them. It was a simple message but soon priests and lay leaders, and even bishops, were being killed because they took the commitment seriously.

Conservatives in the Vatican became alarmed at this breaking of traditional boundaries and began to appoint more moderate bishops to key dioceses but at the next meeting, at Puebla in 1979, the progressives were able to make their voice heard again and proclaimed an 'option for the poor.'

Some of the participants at Puebla came to Knock and gave eye-witness reports. The new challenges were to show solidarity with the people, live with the poor, defend human rights and learn from popular religion.

We even got the Knock Congress on the popular 'Late, Late Show' though the TV presenter, Gay Byrne, introduced that segment by saying, 'I'm sure many of you will turn off your sets when you hear that our next item is a Missionary Congress they are holding in Knock.'

A topic that could have got more attention at Knock was the role of laity in mission. Activities in the Catholic Church generally centred around clergy and Religious who devoted their lives to Church communities or social institutions such as schools and medical hospitals. As long as the emphasis was on establishing parishes and basic health and educational facilities it was inevitable that priests, Sisters and Brothers took the lead. People back home generously supported what was being done by their donations.

The IMU already had a Lay Mission Desk and one of the stories in *Builders of Bridges* was about lay missionaries in Thailand. However the only talk specifically on the role of laity at the Congress was given by a Belgian, August Vanistaendal, Secretary General of the International Federation of Trade Unions and later a Minister of State.

In his presentation he said, 'At present we witness a rather timid beginning of lay participation in missionary activities on a volunteer basis. Responsibilities, tasks and status of lay missionaries are still different from those of religious personnel. In the future these distinctions will become less apparent and might disappear altogether.'

The number of people serving overseas with either an independent Lay Mission organisation or in association with an established missionary society was increasing gradually but their contribution was short-term and more in developmental services than in directly sharing their faith or enabling new Churches to become self-sustaining. In countries like Korea the language barrier provided further difficulties for anyone coming for less than five years.

The Congress generated fresh enthusiasm for mission and plans were made to move the IMU offices from Wellington Road to a more spacious location where people could be invited to gather and pool their resources. I did not expect to be involved in the follow-up to the Congress but shortly after it ended the Executive Secretary, Jack O'Brien, retired and I was asked to take over the post temporally. At the AGM in April 1979 I was appointed Executive Secretary despite my insistence that I was going back to Korea when my two years contract ended. The Congress had outlined the new challenges and I knew that if anything was to be done about them it would not be in an office in Ireland but in a country like Korea.

However, it was in Ireland that I was able to build on my interest in Buddhism.

There was a remarkable absence of readable books on Buddhism in Seoul but not in Dublin. I began to read William Johnston's books on Zen. A Belfast man, whose interest in spirituality had deepened while living in Japan, he wrote a number of 'beginner's guides' introducing casual readers to 'sitting' practices.

I took up Zen style meditation myself and acquired my own wooden prayer stool. The twenty minutes I devoted to the practice every morning were relaxing but I wondered if that was all there was to it. When I heard a 'Zen Retreat' was to be held in a Catholic monastery in Tallaght I signed up. It would be guided by a Buddhist nun, an American, assisted by a Dominican priest.

It was an interesting gathering: an American lady dressed in the habit of a Japanese monk showing ten Irish people how to sit in Japanese style, eat Japanese food (though not very much of it) and copy Japanese Zen practices in a Catholic monastery in Dublin.

Still it provided a taste of what a real Zen retreat is like. Though only a three-day event, sleep was reduced to a few hours at night and 'sitting' went on continuously with only a few short breaks for talks and 'walking meditation.'

The priest who was co-directing the Retreat pointed out that the focus of one's meditation could be the Christian God or the 'nothingness' of Zen. From the Christian perspective such mediation might lead to an interior quietness where the 'Cloud of Unknowing' could be encountered without any distractions.

What I found most useful in Zen was its emphasis on living 'day by day' or 'moment by moment.' Awareness of the present did not mean ignoring the world but brought greater sensitivity to the little events in creation that point to something greater. Worries are set aside, unless there is urgency in dealing with them, and the moment of existence appreciated. There are traces of similar practices in early Christianity but they survived only in the mystical tradition while meditative Buddhism kept them central to its tradition.

Ten Irish Catholics had given up their weekend to join in that Buddhist experience and the number of books on Eastern religions and new age spirituality were expanding on the shelves of bookshops. It was obvious a search was beginning for a deeper spirituality than the official Church provided. The trend supported my belief that when people joined the church in Korea, and they were already doing so in droves, they were doing so not just out of a concern for human rights or to be part of a community but to meet deep heart-felt needs that their current spiritual activity no longer satisfied.

I also learnt from the Zen retreat the degree of commitment that serious Zen practice demands and giving that much time to it was not one of my priorities. However my interest in the practical aspects of Buddhism, how it actually affects thinking and behaviour in Korea, was stronger than ever. How had two thousand years of Buddhism influenced the activity-loving Koreans whose only moments of 'quietness' seemed to be when they were asleep? It was one of the questions it would be easier to answer back in Korea.

Chapter 8
Urban Uprising

I returned to Korea in April 1980. Only two years had elapsed but the situation had changed dramatically. President Park Chung-hee had been assassinated on 26 October 1979 and the army under General Chun Doo-hwan had taken over in a coup on 12 December.

When I was working at the Nunciature in 1968 I had met President Park. A new Vatican Ambassador had arrived and I accompanied him to the Presidential Blue House to present his credentials.

Park was small in height but had the confidence of a general used to commanding. I shook hands with him, instead of bowing in the Korean manner, because diplomatic occasions followed the Western protocol. He said the usual words of greeting and then retired for a few minutes private conversation with the Nuncio. Shortly afterwards we drove the 400 metres back to the Nunciature with full police escort.

I admired Park in those early years. He had come to power in a military coup in 1961 when the country needed firm leadership. He set the economy on the road to industrialisation with his Five Year Plans and built up an infrastructure of roads, railways and energy supplies. Fortunately for Korea he enjoyed the financial support of the United States which wanted the country to be a model of prosperity in contrast to the impoverished Communist North. Park later sent 300,000 troops to Vietnam to fight with the US, getting paid in return as well as gaining valuable military experience and contracts.

However in the early '70s the economy began to slow down and people looked for a greater say in decision making. Park responded by imposing a new constitution: martial law was extended, opposition outlawed and his role as president legalised for years to come.

Soon large-scale demonstrations broke out, beginning in his home southern region and spreading to Seoul. Despite the general unrest, on the evening of Friday 26 October 1979 he left the Blue House for a nearby restaurant with trusted friends including Kim Gae-gyu, head of the Korean CIA, and his security detail.

During the meal in a private room, Kim shot the President and the bodyguards. His motives were never fully explained. Kim claimed he deliberately killed the President because he had become an obstacle to democracy but others said he did it out of personal animosity in a drunken state.

After six weeks of confusion, the army under General Chon Doo-hwan took over on 12 December. Hopes for democracy were quickly crushed and martial law proclaimed. However the demand for wider political rights had built up after Park's death and opposition remained strong. Students and professors who had been expelled from their schools by Park had returned to their colleges, organised student and worker unions and launched a resistance campaign.

This was the situation when I returned to Korea in early 1980.

Already there were daily demonstrations in the streets of Seoul calling for the end of martial law, a minimum wage and freedom of the press. On 15 May, a major gathering in front of Seoul Railway Station drew 100,000 people. Two days later Chon Doo-hwan widened the martial law area, closed the universities, banned political activism and curtailed the press. Twenty-six opposition politicians, including Kim Daejong from the southern Chonnam region, were arrested for instigating disturbances.

By then I had received my next appointment, to Chunghung Dong parish in the southern city of Kwangju where I had worked for a short time as assistant to Tommy Moran. I looked forward to a quiet time there, experiencing traditional provincial life. Instead I walked into an urban uprising.

On 18 May, twenty students gathered outside Chonnam University in Kwangju to protest its closure following the martial law extension. They were opposed by thirty paratroopers who charged into the crowd that gathered. The students retaliated with stones.

Around mid-day the students' numbers increased and they began to move towards the city centre. I was sitting in a bus at the downtown Express Terminal when they stormed past. I thought it was just another demonstration and did not realise that this was the start of what was to be known as the 'Kwangju Incident' or 'Kwangju massacre.' A few days previously I had come down to meet Maurice O'Connor who was preparing to leave Chunghung Dong and arranged a day for me to take over. He suggested I start two weeks later as he had some activities to complete in the parish.

That suited me and I got on the bus back to Seoul looking forward to catching up with my friends in Hwa Yang Ni and Haeng Dang Dong. It was almost another month before I could return.

That afternoon the number of protestors in downtown Kwangju grew to 2,000 but 700 reinforcements from the 7th Brigade of the Korean Army arrived and began clubbing demonstrators and onlookers alike. Office workers and shop owners joined the protestors and the soldiers started firing into the crowd. To defend themselves, the demonstrators raided armouries and police stations for M1 rifles, carbines and light machine guns. A battle began.

On the 22nd May the army retreated, surrounded the city and waited for reinforcements. In Kwangju itself a Citizens Settlement Committee of clergy, professors and lawyers was set up to keep order and begin talks with the army. The city became silent.

Meanwhile in Seoul, to which I had returned, the government suppressed news coverage, merely reporting that communist sympathisers were causing trouble in the south. I met with some of my friends in Hwa Yang Ni that day. When we talked about what was happening in Kwangju, Seo Chong-su, who had been the president of the parish council in my time, began to cry, normally something unthinkable for a Korean man.

Seo Chong-su was from the Cholla province, of which Kwangju was the capital. It was distant from Seoul, largely agricultural and less developed. People there felt looked down on as rustic and untrustworthy. In the old days people who lost the king's favour were exiled there. Jokes were common about backward Cholla people and their distinctive accent. In comparison, neighbouring Gyeongsan province, an ancient enemy, had become a prosperous industrial centre. It was also the region from which most of the politicians and military leaders, like Park and Chon, had come. Cholla's only leader was Kim Daejong and he was already imprisoned in Seoul.

Under government pressure, newspapers and radio stations stirred up the old accusations that southerners were troublemakers and communists, and failed to report what was really happening. The only exception was the popular *Tong-A Ilbo* which got around the ban by stating , 'There is no truth in the rumour that twenty people were shot in Kwangju yesterday,' or, 'There is no truth in the rumour that the army has run amuck in Kwangju and is killing civilians.'

The government soon caught on and forced companies that advertised in the paper to withdraw their support. Ordinary people responded by buying small ads saying, 'Greetings to our friends in Kwangju from Seoul University students,' or 'Best wishes to the southern farmers from the northern cooperative.' Finally the authorities gave the newspaper the choice of conforming or being shut down.

In Kwangju, when the local MBC radio reported that only one person had been killed, a crowd attacked and burnt it.

The Columbans in Seoul knew what was actually happening through reports from the ten men left in Kwangju until the phones were cut off on the 22nd. From then on the only news came from people who managed to escape from the city.

Between the 22nd and the 25th, a blockade stopped people getting into or out of Kwangju. Within the city there was no looting as the people waited anxiously to see what would happen.

On the 26th the army was ready to re-enter Kwangju and the citizens prepared for a last stand. At 4.00 am the following morning, troops from the 5th Division stormed through the streets and easily brushed aside the defences. Control was restored but Kwangju had become the new symbol of protest and inspired pro-democracy groups and demonstrations for the next fifteen years.

There is no agreement on the number of casualties in Kwangju. The government admitted that 144 civilians were killed and 129 wounded during the 'incident' as well as 22 soldiers killed and 109 injured. Others estimated that there were between one and two thousand killed. I was to live there for the next three years and judged the number had been in the hundreds rather than thousands.

When I got to the city in early June, it was quiet but there were strong suppressed emotions. The president of our parish council was one of those arrested. He was the head of the printing department in Chonnam University and students had used copying machines there to print anti-government materials. It was enough that he was responsible for the department but he would also have been sympathetic to the students' cause.

As it happened, the police chief in our district was also a Catholic. His wife was in the Legion of Mary and his university-going son and daughter were members of the choir. However, probably for his own safety, he never appeared at the church until life quietened down and we opened a new building the following year.

It was suggested that we elect a new parish council president since the existing one was in prison but I felt we should show our support and he was still in office when he was eventually released from jail. The majority of the people in the parish approved. The vice-president, a quiet and studious professor at the university, took a risk by not resigning from the parish council and guided us with a steady hand.

As a provincial capital with a population of over a million, Kwangju was an administrative and educational centre and many of our parishioners worked either directly or indirectly for the government as teachers or civil servants. If they took part in anti-government activities they could lose their job. Churches were seen as centres of anti-government activities and with plainclothes policemen at the back of the congregation taking notes, my homilies treaded a narrow line. As a foreigner, I too had to be careful since my residence permit would not be renewed if I was considered too vocally anti-government. A number of missionaries were expelled at that time.

The Korean priests in Kwangju were deeply involved in the demonstrations and a number were imprisoned. Their confreres organised 'prayer meetings' every Monday in one of the parishes and informed us of the location just a few hours beforehand to prevent the police from blocking the entrances.

On one of those occasions I found myself again at the front of a crowd, facing a line of riot police in full gear and armed with batons and tear gas. Their job was to prevent us entering the churchyard. A fellow Columban beside me, usually a mild-mannered man, was pushed to the ground and on the verge of retaliation. The police pressed in on us, with only the grill of their helmets between our faces and theirs. I urged him to hold back as they were mostly young men just as uncertain about what was happening as we were. The young policeman facing us turned away in embarrassment. An officer behind him shouted that he should not be afraid of hitting anyone.

After a while the police retreated a short distance and grounded their shields and batons to form a barrier. An elderly woman, or *halmoni* in the local language, tried to push her way through. When an officer told her to stop she just said, 'I only want to go to the Church to pray,' and, putting her head down, pushed ahead. Eventually he had to let her through; he was not the first to find that a *halmoni* on her way to church was unstoppable.

The 'prayer meetings' were the only public form of protest possible in Kwangju over the next year and it was realistic only for *halmonis*, middle aged women, priests and Sisters to attend. Anyone with a job could lose it and university students could find themselves barred from their studies. Undercover police were everywhere, phones were tapped and printed materials scrutinised to see if there was any anti-government message.

Once a week I went to the bishop's office to help him with his English correspondence. Yun Kong-hee was a quiet man, with the dignity and humility of a true *kunja*. Unlike his friend, Bishop Tji, he was never in jail and led no demonstrations but he gave his priests considerable freedom in organising the 'prayer meetings' and issued measured but clear statements supporting them when necessary. In this low-key approach he followed the example of the highly popular bishop of Seoul, Cardinal Stephen Kim.

It was a year before our parish president was released from jail and the anti-government feeling cooled, but in the meantime our parish life continued along lines which were now common in most of Korea. We had our district leaders and house meetings, the Legion of Mary and various *huis*, a Sunday school, youth groups and a steady stream of young people coming into the Church inspired by the stand of the bishops and priests.

As life returned to normal I looked again at our needs. Like Hwa Yang Ni, the area was a recently developed middle-class area with no nests of poverty. Our energies went into strengthening community spirit and, despite economic stagnation following the Uprising, the people wanted to build a new church or, rather, expand the existing church by constructing a new one alongside.

Ten years previously Chunghung Dong had not existed, it was an area of flat rice fields outside the city. Some of the original farming families remained but the majority had sold their land, got rich and moved out. One of those who had stayed and come to our church to be baptised was given the Christian name, Augustine. Both in appearance and in practice he was a traditional *yangban,* or scholar-farmer in the Confucian manner. He still lived in the family home, a typical thatched farm house with a yard and tall gate that now looked out of place in the suburban setting.

One day when visiting him I shared our plans for expanding the church, now that numbers had increased. I had hoped he would promise a substantial donation but he showed unexpected enthusiasm, suggesting that we set up a 'Church

Building Committee' of which he would be happy to be part. We made him the chairman.

Again the people showed extraordinary generosity. Salaries were tightly controlled and barely covered monthly expenses. For luxuries like new clothes, house repairs, celebrations and repayment of debts the family depended on two yearly bonuses, each worth one month's pay. These were due at the New Year and Autumn Festival. Yet, in Chunghung Dong, like Hwa Yang Ni and Haeng Dang Dong, the people were willing to offer one of the bonuses, the equivalent of a month's earnings, to build a church.

With a response like that the expanded church was built within a year and, six months after that, all the debts had been paid off.

When I moved to Kwangju I had expected to see more of rural life. The city had been given a new face since my time there with Tommy Moran, with straight wide streets and modern buildings. However some of the old traditions remained.

The summer of 1981 was dry and the farmers began to worry about water for their rice paddies. One day I read in the local newspaper that the governor of the province, an ex-army man, had gone with a retinue to the top of Mount Mudung outside the city to perform the traditional *ki-u-che* or 'Praying for Rain Sacrifice.'

This meant climbing the mountain in Confucian ceremonial robes, offering incense and a pig's head, reciting the required formulas and eating a simple meal. It was significant that in a modern city, so soon after a major civilian disturbance, the highest official would feel obliged to carry out this religious ritual. Confucianists felt uneasy about popular religion but early on they saw the need to control all ritual and if praying for rain was included in that they were willing to do it with proper dignity.

Entry to Mudung Mountain was through narrow ravines and some of them were lined with spirit shrines representing Buddhist, Taoist and even more ancient beliefs. Amida stood next to the God of Wealth and further up was the Earth Spirit. There was no competition between them, each brought his or her own spiritual powers and what one did not do, perhaps another would. I found similar valleys in the hills around Seoul when I returned to live there.

Shamanistic celebrations were once more being celebrated on village level, a sign that life in the countryside was almost back to normal after the destruction of the War. Rural communities would put on a week-long festival with different *kuts* each night and shamans came from different parts of the country to participate. The surrounding fields were alive with colourful spirit flags, clouds of smoke from the cooking and clamour of drumming and cymbals.

Such events were intended to renew bonds between villagers, ancestors and local divinities and many family members who had moved away returned for the occasion. I regretted that I knew no one there who could invite me to the celebrations and explain the different dances. The villages were outside the city and none of my parishioners had the time or interest to go to them.

I was in Kwangju for less than three years. By the time I left much of the tension caused by the massacre had lessened though the anniversary of the '5.18 Incident' (18 May), as it was called, continued to be celebrated with bitter feelings. The reputation of the Catholic Church was high as it was seen as standing up for the people. We did not hold any protest meetings in our parish but I participated in those held in the city, encouraged others to attend, read out the bishop's statements and supported our Parish Council president when he was in jail. It was a sign of how much the situation had changed when, on the 33rd anniversary of the 'Incident' in 2013, President Park Geun-hye, daughter of Park Chung-hee, visited the cemetery in Kwangju and said, 'I believe achieving a more mature democracy is a way of repaying the sacrifice paid by those who died.'

***

My stay in Kwangju ended abruptly because I went as a delegate to the 1982 Columban General Assembly and, before it ended, was elected a member of the General Council.

The 1982 Chapter, or Assembly as it was then called, was held in Lima, Peru. Finally I had a chance to see the country in which I had expected to spend my life. In our final year as students the Pope was appealing for priests to go there and we thought of brushing up our Spanish. However none of our classmates were sent to Chile or Peru. If I had gone to Latin America rather than Asia I would undoubtedly have become a different person.

However in 1982 the opportunity finally came to see something of that continent and find out what I had missed.

With the three other representatives from Korea, we went via Los Angeles and Miami to Lima. Up to the 1940s the city had been a typical Spanish-style metropolis with a cathedral, bishop's house and government building facing each other across a Grand Plaza. Then farmers began to come down from the poverty-stricken Andean region in search of jobs and education. First they lived in slums in the centre but then 'land invasions' began on the edges of the city as they moved into unoccupied areas *en masse* and refused to leave. Between 1940 and 1980 the population increased from 600,000 to 4.8 million. The Columbans there worked with the new migrant communities.

We were brought to the Columban Central House at Sol de Oro through dusty streets and past rows of basic mud-brick houses. They said it never rained in Lima and the water came from distant mountains. It was warm at that time of the year but the sun seldom shone through the dust-laden clouds. I was used to buildings rising rapidly in Seoul and Kwangju and asked why so many two-storey houses were unfinished. It seemed people were adding a second floor brick by brick when they had a few pence to spare.

While we were in Lima we did a tour of the historic Inca and pre-Inca sites around the city and during a break in the Assembly we also had a chance to go to the world heritage sites of Cusco and Machu Picchu in the High Andes. That trip took three days as we had to rest for a few hours after arrival to get accustomed to the high altitude. It was worth the effort just to experience the train trip across a mountain ridge to Machu Picchu and walk around the mountaintop fortress.

Those magnificent remnants of Inca culture made me wonder how a highly advanced culture like theirs could disappear in the space of two or three generations. Now the Quechua-speaking people were living in simple mountain huts or shantytown shacks and the Church was only beginning to reach out to them in their ancient language and heritage.

The fact that the assembly was held in Latin America had a strong influence on all the participants. In 1979 the Church there had committed itself to an 'option for the poor' during the Puebla conference. A year later, Bishop Oscar Romero had been killed by gunfire inside his own church because he took that stance in El Salvador.

Columbans were working in both Chile and Peru. In Chile, 2,279 people had 'disappeared' during the Pinochet Regime which began with a coup in 1973. A further 31,947 people were tortured and 1,312 exiled at the same time. The only critical voice to be heard in public was that of the Church where Cardinal Raul Silva took a lead. Columbans fully supported the Cardinal and their house in Santiago had been attacked with gunfire.

In Peru, 70,000 people were to die in a conflict between the government and various Marxist groups including the 'Shining Path' rebels. The Church there was not as united as in Chile, and the situation was more complex, but Columbans worked in the poorest shanty areas and there was no doubt what their option was. Two Australian Sisters in one Columban parish were brutally killed in the plaza of their mountain town.

This concern for human rights and the poor was not limited to Latin America. In the Philippines the Church was mobilising the people against the harsh Ferdinand Marcos regime and in Korea bishops and clergy had been forced to come out against Park Chung-hee and, later, Chon Doo-hwan.

These were not coincidences. Awareness was growing of the international role played by the National Security State system developed in the United States. It was intended to combat the growth of communism around the world and encouraged a central role for the military, suspicion of democratic movements, identifying cunning enemies and restricting public debate in the media.

Western missionaries were seen as 'Leftish' and distrusted. Army and police personnel were trained to implement the national security system and the use of torture when questioning suspects was considered normal.

Many of the dictators were initially successful in promoting industrialisation and brought people into the cities from unsustainable farms to work on building projects or in factories. Those rural migrants came full of hope for the future but soon found themselves trapped in a new form of poverty. With the government changing the laws whenever it suited them, the people were forced to fit into its economic plans, work in low-paid jobs and live in homes without basic amenities.

In Lima, with such dramatic events occurring on their doorstep, the Assembly delegates gave more attention to the political and economic situation than they had at Baguio six years previously.

Once again, those active in Liberation Theology and Basic Communities in Latin America and the Philippines wanted to see a strong commitment to the poor while those working in Korea, Japan and Fiji saw 'liberation' as more than meeting material objectives. Latin America and the Philippines had already been Christianised, or at least had large Catholic populations, and the task there was to build on the gospel tradition already established. However, Christianity was new to the people of Asia where the challenge lay in introducing them to basic Christian beliefs and values. The difference in the two situations was not fully appreciated and made it difficult for one group to acknowledge what the other saw as important.

The document that emerged from the Chapter tried to cover both circumstances. It called for solidarity with the poor, outreach to non-Christians, cultural adaptation and dialogue with other religions. If there was something new it was to make the plight of the poor the basis for everything we said and did.

The debates that produced the document were passionate and in the end neither side fully accepted the importance of the local situation in determining where the priorities should be.

At first I had hopes that the Church's focus on the poor might be the unique aspect of Christianity that missionaries brought to other cultures and religions. In countries where the religious field was shared with Confucianists, Buddhists, Shamans and popular religions, as well as agnostics and atheists, we needed a clear message and identity. That is probably what I was looking for back in Kangjin when the American sergeant asked me what I was doing there. Was this the unique contribution Christianity had to offer?

However I had to admit that the gospel message was more than a social agenda. Emphasising the social commitment element would appeal to the yearnings of young people but even the rebellious citizens of Kwangju would be surprised to hear that an option for the poor was essential to their Christianity. They had recently been poor themselves and knew what it was in practice but the idea that social concern was at the heart of Christianity, rather than the inevitable outcome of it, would appeal neither to their traditional sense of the sacred nor their felt spiritual needs.

In one committee discussion, when I suggested that the new emphasis on the 'option for the poor' might be seen as another Western imposition on the people's traditional religiosity, the idea was not well received. I could see the danger of it becoming another case of outsiders deciding what the local people needed. Yet I believed that the Church should be clearly on the side of the poor and I wanted to do something about it when I got back to Korea.

The other key discussion was equally controversial. There was a proposal that we look for recruits to our Society from all the countries in which we worked.

The long established Religious Orders recruit wherever their members reside so the Order can become part of that country. However, missionary societies did not follow their example. They saw themselves as there to help build up a local diocese with local bishops and priests, and when this was done they moved elsewhere. Recruiting locally would mean staying on permanently and be contrary to that objective.

At the Lima Assembly some of our members were convinced we could learn from new nationalities and it would also provide people in the young Churches with an opportunity to join an international missionary society. Many of the 'young Churches' now had sufficient local priests and Religious to be able to send some abroad. There may also have been an awareness that the number of those joining in our traditional home countries was decreasing and if we wanted new members they would have to come from elsewhere.

Others were conscious that we already were a sometimes uncomfortable mixture of Irish, British, American, Australian and New Zealanders who occasionally had trouble coping with cultural differences. There were complaints that the majority Irish had too much influence. Our ability to embrace other cultures might not be our strong point.

Eventually it was agreed to open membership to applicants from the countries in which we worked.

Towards the end of the Assembly elections were held for a new Superior General and four council members. I was elected as one of the council members which meant I would be based in Ireland for the next six years and be involved in implementing the Chapter's decisions.

Chapter 9
Exploring New Openings

The Central Administration of the Society was based in Dublin but our work meant we would do a lot of travelling. For anyone with a travel bug the prospects looked good. It would mean visiting new countries and cultures and even if I were only a short-term guest, staying with confreres who had lived among the people for many years would provide me with an 'insider's view.' I could compare the situation there with what I had experienced elsewhere.

Each of the four Councillors took on special responsibilities and I managed to avoid everyday tasks like finances, on-going education or implementation of the decision to accept members from different countries. Instead I got the growth areas of new missions, lay mission, China and inculturation and with them a chance to look into the future.

The Assembly had encouraged us to send more people to the areas of Latin America where liberation theology and basic communities had originated and my first trip was to Brazil where many of the new movements had developed. I was accompanied by my colleague, Mike Hoban, who had worked in Chile and spoke fluent Spanish. Our first stop was the north-eastern State of Bahia, known for its poverty and large population of Afro-Brazilians.

On our way there from Rio we stopped off at Recife, a diocese known internationally because of its bishop, Helder Camara. His attitude was expressed by the statement, 'When I gave food to the poor, they called me a saint. When I asked why they are poor, they called me a Communist.' Brazil, like so many developing countries at that time was run by a National Security State government which Dom Helder accused of using violence to suppress demonstrations caused by poverty and injustice.

He was not in Recife when we passed through but we stayed with the Irish Kiltegan Fathers and got their briefing on the situation. We then headed north to Salvador, in Bahia, the first colonial capital of Brazil. Its imposing 'upper city,' perched on an escarpment and looking out over a wide bay, still had traces of its Portuguese origins and past glory. An ancient elevator joined it to the 'lower town' on the water's edge.

The elderly Archbishop of Salvador said he would welcome any priests we could send as he had empty parishes in the poor favela areas. He spoke little English but Mike and himself managed to communicate in a mixture of Spanish and Portuguese.

The bishop encouraged us to visit the Italian Comboni priests who lived in one of the favelas. They had worked in Nigeria previously and were keen to build on the understanding of local religions gained there. The majority of the people have strong links with Africa and the laneways throbbed with the sounds of Candomble, a popular religious sect. I was impressed by the simple life style of the Italian priests and their plans to draw on African religion. Someday I hoped to do something similar in Korea.

We then went inland to Barreiras, a town 853 kilometres west of Salvador. The night bus took over fourteen hours to get there, climbing for a few hours and then motoring through a level, featureless countryside. We had comfortable seats and slept most of the time. Barreiras itself was a disappointment if you were looking for tourist attractions. It had been founded in 1902 with a population of two thousand to service local farms and ranches and had not changed much in the meantime.

The young Swiss bishop, Ricardo Weberberger, was delighted to hear we might have some priests with Latin American experience to send him. The diocese had been set up in 1979, covering an area of 28,000 square miles of bush but had few parishes. He showed us Petropolis, one of the typical communities, and it reminded me of the semi-deserted towns that appeared in Western movies with tumbleweed blowing down the main street and people peeping cautiously out from shaded windows.

The centre of the town was a dusty empty square with a shrine containing at least thirty small statues of saints, a spiritual powerhouse. I had seen an equivalent gathering of statues on the hillsides of Korea but there they were Buddhist, in Petropolis they were Catholic.

There was tension all over the North-East between small farmers, new settlers, loggers and agro-business companies wanting to buy up and clear huge tracts of land. Evictions enforced by posses of mounted and armed men were common. Working there would be lonely and among a different type of poor.

Following our visit, a team of six men was sent to Barreiras and a year later I visited them to see how they were getting on. They had completed their Portuguese studies and were in three rural parishes, including Petropolis. Already they looked part of the 'wild West' setting. One evening ten of us went out for supper in a popular eating house where groups of men sat around long tables drinking beer and eating stripes of meat sliced from smoking skewers brought to them. In the middle of our celebration a rough looking cowboy came over and asked if we were gauchos from Rio Grande do Sul. If we were returning there soon he would like to ride with us. At least it showed our men fitted in well.

The final area we visited on our Brazil trip was on the Amazon River, west of Menaus. The city, 900 miles from the sea, is the 'Heart of the Amazon' and besides an international airport has regular visits from ocean-going ships. Since the time of the Rubber Barons it boasts an Opera House, the Teatro Amazones, to which famous vocalists came by boat from Europe.

However, we were going on to Coari, a town on the Solimoes River, west of Menaus and about ten hours away by boat. Fortunately the bishop, Gutemberg Regis, came in his episcopal barge to escort us. We learnt a lot about the Amazon on the way. The river actually starts near Manaus where the Negro and Solimoes join. We passed the 'meeting of the waters' and the bishop told us the flow was so strong that the dark brown of the Negro and the clear water of the Solimoes did not mix for another five miles downstream. The current of the Amazon itself was so powerful that its flow of fresh water could be tasted two hundred miles out to sea.

The bishop's modest boat could do no more than five miles an hour against the flow so we had plenty of time to view the primeval rainforest as we snaked our way through it. The river split into narrow channels lined with dull green vegetation and, to my disappointment, there was little wildlife or variety in the scenery.

Shortly after a simple lunch on board, the boat turned up a side stream to visit a parish run by American Redemptorist priests. The church was on a small flat island with just room for a chapel, house and basketball court. When a big crowd gathered, Mass would be held outside in the basketball court.

As we continued our journey, one of the priests returning to Coari told me that an annual fiesta was held at the church we had just visited and people from the outstations gathered there to spend a few days celebrating together. Eventually the largest of the outstations built its own church and invited the bishop and priests to come for their first fiesta. The church was too small however and Mass was held outside on a level piece of ground. Afterward a visitor asked one of the locals why there was a basketball post with a hoop behind the altar? Did they play basketball and, if so, why only one post?

'Basketball post?' asked the mystified local.

'Yes, the post behind the altar.'

'Oh, that,' the local replied, 'That has nothing to do with sports. It is one of the fiesta symbols, just as in the parish church.'

Obviously they had seen that strange post when Mass was held in the parish basketball court and thought it was a religious symbol. There was an interesting religious lesson there somewhere.

Coari is a small river town and most of the church work was done by launch or canoe up and down the countless tributaries. I came away with admiration for the catechists and priests who moved from one isolated forest village to another keeping in contact with remote communities.

We went back down the river the following evening, using the overnight public transport boat. The people in Menaus had provided us with hammocks to hang from hooks on the open deck, sharing the space with thirty men and women and with hens and ducks for further company. We were assured there were fewer mosquitoes on the Solimoes and as the boat moved faster downstream insects would not bother us.

Working on the Amazon would be physically challenging and might appeal to the adventurous but we could not see ourselves sending anyone there. They would have little support, cut off by a thousand miles from other Columbans. However we did send a team of seven to Salvador and another to Barreiras, men who had worked in Peru, Chile or the Philippines. Their Spanish would be a help in learning Portuguese and despite the vast distance between them they could meet a number of times a year to plan and socialise together.

Six months later I was in the Caribbean. A number of older men were willing to take on a new challenge but did not want to have to learn a completely new language. English was spoken in many parts of the Caribbean and we visited two of them, Jamaica and Belize. This time l was accompanied by the Superior General, Bernard Cleary, an Australian.

The island of Jamaica is divided into three counties with good English names: Cornwall, Middlesex and Surrey. Surrey is on the eastern end and its capital is the famous or infamous city of Kingston. Once a pirate lair, its reputation has not improved over the years.

At the other end of the island is the tourist enclave of Montego Bay. It developed late and only in 1967 was a diocese established there with Edgerton Clarke as the first bishop. Almost twenty years later he still had only four priests and he was eager for Columbans to staff parishes along the coast and in the less populated hinterland.

The bishop met us at the new international airport and brought us to his cathedral on a hill at the edge of the town. The weather was warm, the beaches white and the scenery a lush green but I never felt relaxed. Whatever about being a paradise for tourists, it would not be one for church workers.

Montego Bay itself was comparatively peaceful and the beaches were cordoned off to encourage locals to stay out. However inland the sight of crashed single-engine planes, nose down in the earth, was not uncommon. They had been used to smuggle drugs off the island.

Large numbers of African slaves had been brought to the island for the sugar industry and they achieved freedom only in 1838 after a series of rebellions. Inter-racial relationships were still delicate. The country became independent in 1962 and when the economy began to deteriorate in the 1970s inequality and poverty became widespread. Missionaries going to work there would be faced with economic stagnation, crime and family instability. One of the men we sent there was later stabbed to death. The percentage of other Christian denominations was high, with strong African influences on their preaching and singing. Catholics numbered only 2%.

The local people spoke some English--the reason we considered sending older men there--but usually it was in the form of an English-African Creole language called Jamaican Patois which would take some getting used to. Montego Bay was a challenge, even for men with previous overseas experience.

Finally we went to Belize. Again, the reason was because one of its official languages was English. Belize is a tiny country on the north-east coast of Central America and from 1500 BC to 900 AD was part of the Mayan Empire. Today the Mayan ruins at Caracol and Xunantunich are among its few tourist attractions.

The country became a Crown Colony in 1862, called British Honduras, at a time when the London government sought to gain control over the English and Scottish pirates who had settled there and were known as the Baymen. They continued their pirate trade for many years and also exploited the forests for hardwood. Today Belize has a population of only 350,000 and besides tourism its main claims to fame is that it is the birthplace of chewing gum.

It was an unlikely place to start a new mission but, understandably, there was a shortage of priests. Earlier in its history the majority of the people had been Catholic but Protestant and other missionaries had arrived over the previous twenty years and now only 40% were considered Catholics.

The bishop, Osmond Peter Martin, drove us 80 km along the brand new highway from Belize City to the capital, Belmopan. Belize City had almost been flattened by the 300 miles-an-hour winds of Hurricane Hattie in 1961 so the government had decided to build a brand new capital inland where it would be safer. Belmopan might be better protected from the elements but in terms of beauty it is in no danger of putting the Mayan cites in the shade. After a quick look around we returned through the still heavily wooded countryside to Belize City.

The local people were undoubtedly poor and integrating themselves into their culture, an Afro-British mix, would not be easy for whoever we sent. However, we eventually decided to send a small team there also. Both in Belize and in Jamaica the plan was for our men to stay just ten years and in that period to do their best to make the local Church more self-sustaining.

During our visits to Brazil and the Caribbean I realised that the supply of local priests was not likely to increase in the near future and many communities would never have a traditional form of parish. The laity needed to take on, and be given, more responsibility and we hoped that our men from Chile and Peru who were experienced in training local leaders would help find a remedy.

A serious cultural challenge also faced them. Because of slavery, the African influence was strong especially in the area of religion and the official Church was more inclined to condemn 'superstitious practices' in Candomble than look for positive features. Immersed in the daily poverty and drug scene, the Caribbean would be no holiday for the men going there.

* * *

There was a feeling of reliving the pioneering days in setting up those new missions but in fact I was having a grandstand view of the final stages of traditional missionary expansion. The age of going abroad to supply young churches with foreign personnel, mainly priests to take care of parishes and other essential services, was over. Local resources were now stronger and the number of long-term missionaries diminishing.

However, my other responsibilities involved me in activities that would define the future in a more confident way.

With the number of clerical and Religious missionaries declining, who would replace them? One of my jobs was to get lay (non-clerical) involvement in mission off the ground.

The first step we took was to employ a layman to coordinate the program. From my IMU days I had known Chuck Laytrop, an American who had been director of the Maryknoll Fathers Lay Mission Program in the U.S and had just completed a survey on lay mission in Europe. Chuck took up the post but left for family reasons after a year and I succeeded him as the role was not very demanding at that stage.

Before he left, Chuck and myself visited the Philippines to stir up interest and were in the southern island of Negros in 1983 when two of the 'Negros Nine', Niall O'Brien and Brian Gore, were there under house arrest. They attended our meeting but their minds may have been elsewhere as they were being accused of murdering the local mayor and under threat of a death sentence. The trumped-up charges were an effort to blacken their names and halt their efforts to support local sugar workers. Their case attracted international attention, especially in Ireland and Australia, and happily came to a conclusion a year later when they were cleared of all charges.

Back in Dublin we drew up a four-page lay mission policy and invited the various regions in which our men worked to send or receive a lay team. There was no immediate response as nearly all our members worked in parishes or church activities where they already had plenty of local lay volunteers. Finding short-term work for foreign lay missionaries would be difficult enough, and when language studies and time to adjust to the culture were taken into consideration, it was too great a commitment to take on immediately. The program got off to a slow start.

Japan was the first to come up with a request. Our men there could place three teachers in an international school in Tokyo where they would teach religious studies among other subjects. It was not ideal, even if they would be teaching children of twenty different nationalities, but at least they would not have to face the daunting task of learning Japanese. I contacted Teacher Training Colleges in Ireland, got some names, interviewed the teachers and sent three off to Tokyo that autumn with a minimum of preparation. The following year I enrolled three more and the program was up and running.

The only other achievement was to send two ex-army men from Ireland to Pakistan, one as a mechanic and the other as a builder. At least the program was launched and our members were gradually getting used to the idea. Later, when I returned to Korea, I was asked to start the program there and had more success.

Another of my responsibilities was China. Our Society had been founded in 1918 as 'The Maynooth Mission to China' and up to 1954, when the last Columban was expelled from there, China had been our main focus.

During the following thirty years it was impossible to enter China, or get any reliable news of what happened in the areas where we had worked. However we had 'China Watchers' in Hong Kong keeping in touch with a number of contacts inside and following developments.

In 1984 I was invited to an ecumenical China Conference outside London at which three Protestant ministers from mainland China attended. One was a smartly dressed young man who spoke good English and the other two were older men in Mao suits. We soon discovered that the young man, the son of an Anglican bishop, would only recite the fixed Party line when questioned. According to him there was religious freedom in China and no persecution of Christians. The older men, on the other hand, if approached in a quiet corner, would confide that the situation was still not good though it was improving slightly.

China had changed more than I realised. After Mao's death the country opened slowly to the outside world and there were possibilities of working there again. Missionaries were not welcome as such--for historical reasons they were seen as a colonial and westernising body--but if anyone had a skill or commercial opportunity to offer they were acceptable. A Chinese-American Christian group, Amity, was sending English teachers to universities there, building a printing press for bibles and supporting welfare projects.

In early 1983 I visited Hong Kong and stayed with our 'China Watcher,' Edward Kelly, who had begun trips into the areas where the Columbans had worked to find out about conditions there. He encouraged me to go on a one-day tour from Hong Kong to nearby Zhuhai through Macao. Among the places we visited were the home of Sun Yat-sen, the great Chinese revolutionary and 'Father of the (Modern) Nation,' and the first golf club to be built since Mao's time. Ironically it was called 'Mission Hills' and was eventually to become the biggest golf complex in the world with twelve 18-hole courses.

Our bus stopped for a while in Zhuhai town, then a rural market, and crowds of beggars surrounded the vehicle, tapping aggressively at the windows, asking for money.

Encouraged by the signs of a reopening in China, I got my fellow Council members to agree to setting up a new commission to keep track of what was happening and encourage the men in neighbouring Japan, Korea, Taiwan and the Philippines to get involved.

A year later, Edward Kelly and myself were the first Columbans to return to Nancheng, in Jiangxi province, the second diocese the Society had staffed in China. We went as tourists and had to wait three days in the provincial capital to get an 'inland visa' as the town we wanted to visit was in a restricted area. Our official reason for going was to find the grave of 'an uncle' of mine who had been a missionary there long ago. In fact there were a number of Columbans buried in the province and the location of some of the graves was still unknown.

We hired a car for the four-day journey and were accompanied by a driver and a young guide from the Tourist Office. Whenever we got to a town whose name Ed recognised, we got out to stretch and gaze around to see if there were any church steeples on the horizon. We located quite a few but when we approached them usually no one could, or would, tell us what denomination they belonged to.

There were no hotels, maybe that was the reason the area was 'restricted,' so we stayed in the Communist Party Guest Houses. When we got to Nancheng and were given a room I looked out the window and there, right across the road, was Bishop Patrick Cleary's cathedral which no Columban had seen for more than thirty years. We pretended to show only casual interest but were told we could not go in since it was used as a factory.

Shortly afterward Ed Kelly set up an organisation similar to Amity's, called AITECE, to send teachers to China. Later I would be its manager.

***

Another new area whose importance was gradually being accepted was inculturation, that is, helping to find roots in the local culture and religions from which the local Church could draw meaning and energy. Cultural sensitivity had not been part of our Columban training and was not a high priority for reasons mentioned already. Indeed the concept was comparatively new and there was still little agreement on what it meant in practice. Some just saw it as using the local language and aspect of religious traditions to made Christianity more easily understood. Others believed it was not necessary at all as most of the people we worked with wanted a fresh modern outlook and often showed little regard for their own traditional religions.

However I was becoming more aware that one of unique aspects of Christianity was its historical concern not to be associated with any one culture since its message was meant for all cultures. That is what brought it out from under the shelter of Judaism and into the Greek and Roman worlds. It also found roots in the cultures of Persia, the Middle East and North Africa as well as Eastern Europe, before efforts were made to restrict it to a Western, or Greco-Roman, expression. People were wakening up to the fact that the original mission of Christianity was to find expression in African, Latin American and Asian cultures while retaining its own core vision. It would take time for Church leaders to take up this challenge again but a start was being made.

Not unexpectedly, our own members felt little sense of urgency. I tried to stir up interest by writing articles and organising seminars but soon realised I would have to wait until I returned to Korea to explore what it meant in practice and what we, as foreigners, could do.

Meanwhile, I prepared by reading up on religions and cultures. In the different countries I visited I could see similarities in symbols and practices. It was as if there had once been a universal religion, a common awareness of the sacred in the world, which sprung from the human DNA and expressed itself creatively in remarkably similar ways.

In Pakistan I saw men walking in circles around the graves of the holy men in a shrine in Lahore, carrying candles and murmuring prayers, just as I had seen Catholics in the Philippines performing the same activities around the statue of Santo Nino, the Child Jesus, in Cebu. In Ireland we had 'the patterns.'

In Korea I saw thorn trees beside sacred wells with pieces of cloth hung on them by people looking for cures. The exact same practices can be found in Ireland. Water, rocks, mountains, fire, caves, trees, the moon and the sun are sacred symbols everywhere and New Year rituals of death and revival follow the same pattern in almost every civilisation.

Why was this sense of the sacred dying out in Europe?

In the age before 'google' I visited libraries and bought books to find the answer. It seems that the first significant change came when the 'great religions'--Zoroastrian, Hebrew and Confucian–evolved, focussing on one heavenly God and in the process moving a wider sense of sacred presence into the background. The previous gods, spirits and religious practices were abolished or submerged because they were a distraction. As a result, the awareness of a sacred presence was directed more 'up there' than 'down here.'

The next shift was in the 17th century when the Age of Reason, or the Enlightenment, demanded the study of religion to be scientific and rational. Since neither God nor the Sacred can be measured mathematically, religion was pushed further into the background and a range of beliefs from scepticism to atheism to fundamentalism emerged. When industrialisation promoted the importance of enjoying, and showing-off, material wealth, the challenge from a less physical but equally powerful counter-message was further downplayed.

As I had discovered, the Orient had escaped this alienation. There, and elsewhere outside Europe, religion is still a respected reality. Visiting Westerners can be surprised by the people's familiarity with the sacred and react to it by seeing it as disagreeable and outdated, curious but vaguely familiar or inspirational and a rediscovery.

Before my six years on the General Council ended I gathered my findings in a book and sent it to a number of publishers under the title, *In Search of the Sacred*. Only one replied, pointing out that most of my material was second-hand. I took the point and accepted that if I wanted to go any further with the search I would have to do it among real people, not books, and Korea was the best place to try.

In 1988, our next General Assembly would be held in Busan, Korea, and I packed to be back in time for the Seoul Olympics which were held around the same time. I took my basic belongings with me, knowing I would stay. It was time to fill out the answers to those questions that now had a clearer shape in my mind.

Chapter 10
Moon Village Squatter

Back again to Seoul, arriving in the middle of Olympic excitement. I got there just in time to see 'Flo-Jo' Joyner win two gold medals. Korea too was flying and felt it had finally arrived as a seriously advanced country. I looked forward to getting involved in what would happen next but first there was the General Assembly.

This time the gathering was in southern city of Busan but, unlike the meeting in Lima, its location in a suburban retreat house did little to influence the proceedings. Those coming to Korea for the first time had few opportunities to feel what was really happening in the country though they were impressed by the modernity, success in hosting the Olympics and evident energy of the Church. There was nothing like the poverty of Peru or the innovative thinking of the Latin American theologians to stimulate fresh ideas. The cultural challenges which the Korean, and other Asian, Churches faced were not so obvious.

General Assemblies (previously known as General Chapters) were held every six years and this was the third I attended. For me the novelty had worn off and the tension of the Baguio and Lima gatherings was lacking. Maybe the membership was getting older and there was greater tolerance of conflicting viewpoints.

This time, besides repeating the call to be with the poor, pay more attention to local religious traditions and encourage lay people to get involved in mission, the gathering drew attention to the re-opening of China, the demands of becoming an international Society with members from different cultures and the urgency of growing ecological concerns.

The challenges put to the members called for an urgent response but it was left to each region or country to meet them as best their resources, and situation, allowed. I had been involved in planning some of the new programs, now I wanted a part in implementing them.

As soon as the Assembly ended I headed for Seoul with a good idea of what I wanted to do but unsure how I could put my hopes into practice.

The Korea to which I returned had become accustomed to daily demonstrations, often violent, and the taste of tear gas. Behind the 'demos,' as they were called, the issues were both political and economic: strong pro-democracy and anti-American feelings as well as calls for independent trade unions and compensation for relocating families as urban redevelopment began. An underlying tension caught my attention. While Westernisation promised greater personal freedom and satisfaction, the legacy of Confucius was continuing to make conflicting family and social demands. The young demonstrators calling for greater democracy and human rights also feared that the attractive Western ways might be destroying their cherished national distinctiveness.

I wanted to be close to the search for a new national identity but if I worked in traditional parish structures my involvement with people would be limited. As I had found in my previous assignments, living in a church compound, in basically Western style, created barriers.

Fortunately I heard that a Columban, Noel Daly, had a few years previously gone to a shanty town area in western Seoul, Shillim Dong, on weekends. Two other men, Chris Farrelly and Noel Mackey, eventually moved there, renting a shack to live among the people. Over the next four years, along with local helpers, they studied the needs of the area and built up community social and medical services.

Noel and Chris were due to leave there the following April so I volunteered to take their place. In the meantime I could give time to some of my other interests.

Studying Korean is a never-ending challenge so I enrolled for a refresher course run by the Maryknoll Fathers in their house near Hwa Yang Ni. Their approach was based on watching tapes of a popular TV drama, memorizing all the parts in the script overnight and repeating them in front of the teacher and the silenced TV the next day. I not only learnt new popular expressions but got hooked on the dramas which was a help later when working with the women of Shillim 10.

In the New Year, I joined the Inculturation Centre that another of our men, Sean Dwan, had started in Wangsipni, researching Korean culture and producing a quarterly magazine entitled, *Inculturation.*

I felt that adapting Christianity to the local culture should be attempted 'in the field' rather than in a library but I spent the next few months usefully, researching recent Korean religious developments and writing articles for the magazine. When Sean left Korea for another assignment I took his place. I reduced the magazine to a bi-monthly newsletter based on articles I translated from local papers and magazines including *The Religious Times*, a useful publication from the Unification Church. There were also interviews I did with Korean experts in the field of culture and religion.

It was an exciting time for religion in Korea. A group called the Dami Mission announced that the world would come to end on 28 October 1992. On that 'Day of Rapture' God's angel would pass over the earth and snatch up those with raised hands, while those who were not prepared would perish. People gave up their jobs and students left school. Often when I travelled across Seoul on the mass transit system, teenagers would stand up and urge everyone to sell all they had and prepare for the end.

The movement attracted world-wide attention and the articles I translated from the local papers on the 'Mission for the Coming Days' were avidly studied by universities in the United States and Great Britain.

The world press gathered in Seoul on the night of the 28 October and recorded the disappointment of the 20,000 believers who were left waiting to be 'snatched up.'

By then I was already installed in Shillim 10 and living on my own mountain-top. If love at first sight is meeting face-to-face with an ideal you had in the back of your imagination, then that is what happened to me when I first saw that squatter area on the slopes of Mt Kwanak, in western Seoul.

To call it a squatter area, however, did it an injustice. Latin America had its favelas and barrios, Africa had its shanty towns and townships but Seoul had its unique *tal-tongnae*. These so-called 'moon villages' were located on the side or top of hills. This meant the residents were living close to the sky and had a good view of the moon, hence the name. Normally the moon is associated with harvests and rural life, and most of the inhabitants of the *tal-tongnae* had once worked the soil, but now the moon was just a reminder of their up-rootedness.

The *tal-tongnae* were created by the Korean War which not only caused the death of two million civilians and another two million combatants but forced hundreds of thousands of refugees to stream south in search of safety. With no hope of returning to their farms in the North and no unoccupied agricultural land in the south, they had to find new ways of survival.

Most of them ended up in the capital, Seoul, impoverished but prepared to work long hours for low wages. They settled on waste land in the down-town area and on the banks of the streams that meandered through the capital. When the economy improved and developers wanted to build on the more central locations, the squatters were forced to move out beyond the existing city limits. Without realizing it they were laying the foundations for a modern mega-city which would prosper from their persistence and energy.

Pamgol was the area in which I would live. Its name meant 'Chestnut Ravine' but the trees were long gone and a canopy of shacks covered the banks of its stream. It was part of Seoul's Shillim District that began at the transport-hub around Shillim crossroads and spread back up into the slopes of Kwanak Mountain. One by one the narrow ravines leading into the hills were occupied. Our ravine and the one beside it were designated 'Shillim 10', the tenth civil division of Shillim District.

Halfway up the narrow lane which was the main thoroughfare of Pamgol, stood the 'House of Love' and my new home beside it.

Years later, when I was in Hong Kong, I was tempted to write a novel based on Shillim 10 and its residents but gave up because it seemed a betrayal of trust. The people had shared their hopes and lives so openly with me I felt I would be breaking that confidence by telling their stories, even if I used fictional names. However, my 'never-to-be-finished novel' began by describing the progress of the main character (me) as he journeyed from the No 22 bus terminus towards his home.

'One side of the laneway was cut into the hillside and two women were chatting above him as they weeded their tiny vegetable plots. They quieted as he passed. His house, with its faded blue hut-like toilet across the lane from it, came into view. Unlike the other gates along the passage his was open, to welcome visitors.

'Inside the entrance, on the left, was a small room about ten feet square. As in most Korean homes, its floor was raised and needed an outside step to help people enter. Originally the house had been occupied by two families, one in the front room and one in the double room at the back with both sharing the same kitchen. The Credit Union now used the front room while he lived in the back. The inside courtyard was large, twice the size of the Credit Union office, and had a hand-operated pump in the centre which was useful on 'meals-on-wheels' days. At the far end was the kitchen on a lower level than the courtyard to allow for the *ondol* heating system.

'Because of its freezing winters Korea had developed its own house warming methods, used by both rich and poor. Channels under the floor enabled heated air to pass beneath the rooms to warm them. Originally the heat was created by burning wood in the kitchen which had to be on a lower level. People took off their shoes on entering a room not only to keep it clean but in case they might break the fragile oil paper flooring. To damage it would be fatal because coal briquettes had replaced wood as the fuel and carbon monoxide, known as the 'silent killer', could escape through a cracked channel into the room and kill the occupants before they had any warning.

'His house had one of the safer "New Community Boilers" in the kitchen. It was developed by the government in response to the hundreds of deaths from gas poisoning each winter. Rather than circulate smoke under the floor it piped water from a small boiler. At this time of the year central heating was not needed but the boiler still provided hot water for cooking and bathroom use. The kitchen was also used as the bathroom and taking a shower meant splashing hot or cold water from a plastic dipper. There was a hole in a corner to let the water escape.'

The other room, divided in two by sliding doors, was where I lived, worked, dined and slept.

I was there only a few days when a delegation of local Catholics came to express their concern. The toilet was outside, across the laneway and standing alone like a windowless telephone kiosk. It had no plumbing, just a barrel sunk in the ground. Every month or so the 'night-soil men' would come when it was dark and empty the barrel covertly as such facilities were illegal. There was no seat such as Westerners used, one just squatted.

The locals feared that I was not used to squatting and at my age might get a heart attack if I depended on the existing facilities. Should they get a Western toilet for me? I was 51 at the time and must have looked old to them. I replied that I was quite happy with the present arrangement. Any concern I had was about having to go outside and across the alley to use it during the night or on an icy winter's evening. They were relieved that I didn't want any changes, it seemed right that their priest lived exactly like the locals. Later I was to say that I saw the arrangement as possibly giving me 'squatter rights' in an area where evictions and dispossession were common! I did not mention that at the time as the Confucian attitude was to keep your words sincere, which did not allow much room for puns or a jocose attitude.

I liked the simplicity of Korean living. At night I took the mattress and bed clothes out of a cupboard and laid them on the floor. In the morning I rolled them up again and put them back in their place. There was no need for tables and chairs.

Everyone sat on the floor or on a cushion and when a table was needed at mealtime it was handed in through the hatch and taken away again afterwards.

A neighbouring lady, Julianna, turned up late in the morning to cook lunch and supper for me and tidy up the rooms. She also kept me in touch with the gossip and politics of the area as her family was one of the first to settle there. Typical of the local women, she was full of life and cheerfulness and without her I doubt if I or my predecessors could have survived there.

Whenever she had something new to show me or a special guest arrived, the sliding door would open and she would appear with a, 'Ta-daa.' Otherwise I would communicate with her through the hatch from which my meals would be handed in from the kitchen.

Soon I was like a member of her family, invited to celebrations at her house in the lane behind ours or to picnics with them in the hills above.

When people visited me and asked what I did there, I would say that all I did was sit on the *ondol* floor all day, have tea with visitors and direct those volunteering to help towards what I thought would suit them.

We had a Credit Union in the front room of the house. The chairperson was a very able lady who ran a pharmacy at the bottom of Area B, the neighboring ravine, and Columba Chang took care of the book-keeping. Columba was from outside the district but had volunteered to work in 'The House of Love,' as our community centre was known. After I was there a year I launched the Columban Lay Mission program and Columba was one of the first volunteers. She went on to work in the Philippines with AIDS patients and later in Burma (Myanmar) and set an example of simple living and service that few could equal.

Most of the work in the 'House of Love' community was done by locals, mainly women. However outsiders were also involved. St Mary's Hospital in the city centre, founded by the brother of Paul Yun of Haeng Dang Dong, provided a free general clinic three Saturdays a month. On the fourth Saturday a team came from the Catholic Dental College and we had our own second-hand dental equipment, including an X-ray machine. Once a month, on a Thursday evening, there was a genecology clinic. Local people set up the treatment rooms and took care of registration while the clinic teams were medical students and their professor.

We also had a close relationship with the Joseph Clinic, near Shillim crossroads, run by a young doctor named Sunwon Kyung-Shik, later to become famous as, 'The Champion of the Homeless.' He gave free medical treatment to patients from our area and what he achieved for the poor in that part of Seoul put our efforts in the shade.

The medical clinic was held in 'The House of Love,' a shed-like building beside Julianna's house. We also used it for Mass on weekdays, area meetings and a Sunday School class. It was too small for the people coming to Sunday Masses so we availed of the basement in a building near the bus stop. Breaking all fire regulations, the basement had no windows and only the stairway and a chimney-like affair to circulate air. It was like a sauna in summer when we had three Masses on Sundays with over four hundred people attending.

Every Tuesday morning our little yard was busy with local women cooking rice and soup. Around midday they were joined by the 'downtown ladies' who would bring tasty side dishes from their well-off homes. We would all go off together, up and down the nearby hills visiting those too old or sick to look after themselves. This was 'meals-on-wheels' where no wheels could go. When we had finished our rounds we would sit down in my room for lunch together. The give-and-take between the locals and the 'downtown ladies' broke down all barriers. With money which the 'ladies' provided we also paid for the school lunch for thirty local children.

Up in Area B we had an *aga-bang* or daycare centre for small children, so their mothers could go to work. It was run by Agnes and Maria, two girls in their early thirties. Agnes had two MAs and left a job as a nutritionist in a 4-star hotel downtown to come to Shillim 10. Maria was a tall, graceful girl whose formal education was not equal to Agnes's but she had a natural interest in children and had postponed thoughts of marriage to work there.

The *aga-bang* was on the next ridge to Pamgol, in Area B, near the top of the hill. It was housed in a large shack with one large room downstairs and an attic above in which the two girls slept.

Every Tuesday night we had a Mass in the *aga-bang* and even though it might mean climbing over an ice covered hill to get there in winter, I never liked to miss the occasion. At that time I was writing a column for the monthly *Town and City Magazine*, run by the Church, and in it compared our *aga-bang* Mass with the formal Korean Mass celebrated with a traditional orchestra in the Cathedral.

The Cathedral Mass with its solemnity, traditional instruments and Confucian court music was hailed as a noteworthy effort towards inculturating the Catholic Church but I proposed our Tuesday night liturgy in Area B as a better example. In ours, we all sat on the floor, the altar was a low table, the congregation consisted mostly of local working women with a sprinkling of children. They did the singing and readings and after I said a few words on the gospel they joined in with their own interpretations. In the prayers afterwards everyone, young and old, joined in. When the liturgy ended we continued to sit around for another thirty or forty minutes, nibbling on biscuits and sipping sweetened water while we discuss what was happening locally.

We also had monthly area meetings in homes and early on I made an effort to include some Bible study, feeling the Korean Church in general was lacking in that area. The women were enthusiastic about the idea but once the word 'miracle' came up in the text a lively discussion immediately broke out about a cure at a charismatic meeting the previous week, a local girl who had been possessed by a spirit or shoes that had mysteriously moved from the doorstep to the roof of the house next door. After about twenty minutes of this I would say, 'Now let's get back to what St Luke was saying,' but despite our best efforts talk would soon drift back to other unearthly happenings in the locality.

It made me wonder about the value of formal teaching.

The usual introduction to the Church for newcomers was theological in content and followed Western reasoning patterns. During a session for adults preparing for baptism, I was having trouble explaining in Korean that the Mass was both sacrament and sacrifice. Afterwards one man came up, put his hand on my shoulder and said, 'Don't worry, Father, we believe it whatever it is.'

I wondered if efforts to deepen people's faith can succeed if they are not based on the person's previous religious experience and seen as a way of life rather than a way of knowing. There is something to be said for the traditional approach in communities where people learnt from what they saw others doing and saying.

However, offering prayers came naturally. The women in particular showed no hesitation in seeking blessings not only for their own family but for non-Catholic neighbours and people who were worse off than themselves. They also had the ability to include the humorous side of human squabbles and foibles in their petitions.

If this description of the 'House of Love' is detailed it is not just because I spent what was probably the most satisfying period of my life there, but also because I came to see it as a model of what a real community can be like. While it had a life and rhythm of its own it did not shut out the harsh reality around it. Pamgol existed because of a housing problem and our community joined in the struggle to solve it.

All the resident of Shillim 10 knew the distrust and anxiety that the daily threat of displacement and homelessness cause. But even that conflict had its upside in bringing people together and creating a sense of common struggle. Without the wider context of redevelopment or *chae-kebal* the community might have become self-engrossed, which is not a desirable fate for any group that came together to support each other and their neighbours.

Chapter 11
The House of Love

S hillim 10 came into existence as a temporary solution to a lack of housing and it survived unchanged as long as the need for proper housing was unmet. Every day the thought must have occurred to the residents, 'How long will we be here? What will happen us when redevelopment begins?'

As the Korean economy improved the housing situation got more attention. The city population had grown to eight million. Most of the families displaced in the War settled on the banks of the streams downtown and on hills around the city. They built shacks with whatever materials they could find and put up with a lack of facilities. Dwellings had to be substantial enough to cope with the icy winters when the Capital's Han River froze over and fuel was scarce. Now that expectations were rising the problem could no longer be ignored.

The authorities were also conscious of the city's international image and before the 1988 Olympics they began demolishing unsightly shacks between the airport and downtown. Those that could not be removed were blocked from sight by tall fencing. However the government had to find a long-term solution and launched a redevelopment program, *chae-kebal* in Korean. Squatter areas would be leveled and thirty-storey apartment blocks erected in their place. Already I had seen the results in Haeng Dang Dong. Now it was the turn of the areas further out, like Shillim Dong.

The difficulty was in compensating the shack dwellers. Some of them owned their house, though not the ground on which it was built. After all, they were squatters. The government recognized this reality and allowed the houses to be sold and bought legally, but not the land they were on. We owned the house I occupied and the 'House of Love' but not their sites, so the government could evict us at any moment. The city did offer to compensate the householders by giving them a small apartment elsewhere, a share in an apartment in the same area or a modest lump sum.

However, not all the shack dwellers owned their house, some rented them or leased them under the unique Korean *chon-sae* system. A new tenant would give the owner a lump sum, roughly a tenth of the value of the property, and it would be returned to him or her in its entirety when they left. In the meantime the owner would invest the *chon-sae* money and earn interest on it. But what would happen to the tenant if the house owner sold out? Would they get their deposit back? The answer was not clear and each area had to work out its own solution.

By the time I got to Shillim 10, much of upper Pamgol had already been levelled and work was about to begin on the other side of the hill, in Area B. I soon got accustomed to the noisy meetings and demonstrations as developers, house owners and house tenants forcefully stated their settlement term or claims.

Near the top of Pamgol hill one house still survived, defended by its family members and their relatives. They were Catholics so I visited them occasionally and couldn't but wonder whether they were heroes, combatting City Hall and greedy developers, or just hanging on to get better compensation.

If a householder sold out early he or she could get a good price from the developer who was waiting for just such an opening but that also put pressure on neighbours to sell though they would be offered a lower price. If someone persisted in holding out they could slow up the building project and those who had moved might have to wait to get their compensation. Everywhere there were rumours and suspicion.

We had prominent Catholics on both sides but most of our community were householders or tenants and my sympathy was with them. As the only foreigner living in the area, and as a Church person, normally I would have been excluded from the discussions as had happened to me in previous parishes. In Shillim 10 I found a way to get involved.

From the beginning relationships with other religious groups in the area were good, in particular with a young Presbyterian minister in Area B and two young Buddhist monks belonging to the *Won-Bul* sect.

The two Buddhist monks came from the southern Cholla province which also happened to be the birthplace of their order's founder, Pak Chung-bin. Pak had set out to reform and modernize Buddhism in 1924 but his ideas did not have much impact until after the Japanese occupation of Korea ended in 1945. The emblem he used as a focus for meditation was a black circle on a white field–the Korean word for circle is *won*, hence the name of the order.

Won Buddhists believe in 'timeless and placeless' devotion, emphasising that the Buddha was to be served always and everywhere. Since the beginning of the Yi dynasty, when Buddhism fell out of favor and Confucianism ruled, Korean Buddhists had withdrawn to the mountains and kept out of social involvement. Founder Pak wanted to change that and encouraged his followers to return to the cities and start charitable projects among the disadvantaged. Usually they worked out of monasteries but recently, as an experiment, they had allowed Kim *Kyomunim* and Oh *Kyomunim* to live in a shack in Area B where I first encountered them. *Kyomunim* is the title given to the monks and means 'Honorable Servant of the Doctrine.'

Both of them were tall, thin, active young men. They wore a modern, tighter-fitting version of the traditional Korean overlapping grey vest and the usual baggy trousers of monks. Oh *Kyomunim's* round shaven head gave him the ascetical appearance of a traditional monk while Kim *Kyomunim's* long and alert face hinted at his background as a research student and scholar.

Kyomunims were allowed to marry but could visit their partners only one day a month. This was because they were supposed to put their work above all private and family considerations. Kim *Kyomunim* had been married recently but I never met his wife. He was known for his skill with the *piri*, or Korean flute and had just finished his Masters in sociology. He was thinking of going on to do his doctorate.

The young Presbyterian Minister, Pastor Kim, came from a background with which I was more familiar. He was married and had young children but lived outside the area, coming every day to Area B where he had a small church and community. His father, who had been among the first to move into the district, had built the original church. He still lived nearby, in a small farmhouse on the side of Kwanak Mountain.

Young Pastor Kim kept up the family commitment to Area B. He was serious, neatly dressed and had graduated from one of the more well-known Bible Schools. I came to admire his dedication and asked him one day whether we could collaborate, with the *Kyomunims,* to be of service to the Area B community. It would present a united religious front against accusations that the religions were always fighting among themselves.

Together with the *Kyomunims* we founded the 'Love the Neighborhood Society' (it sounded better in Korean). Our meetings began with three minutes of silence so each participant could pray in his own way without disturbing the others.

As a distinct and potentially influential group we soon got recognition from the local government and the developers, both were willing to come to talk with us. We probably did not change their approach much but at least we could get reliable information about their plans and relay it back to our people to offset some of the rumors.

We cooperated in other areas also. The 'House of Love' had another shack in Pamgol which was no longer used by the clinics so we loaned it to the *Kyomunims* as short-term accommodation for young ex-prisoners. There was some grumbling among a few of our own people, who maybe had an eye on it for themselves, but the majority saw it as a positive move.

That Spring we decided to organize a *Dano Day* celebration in Area B to improve community relations.

Dano is a traditional festival on the fifth day of the fifth lunar month. In Korea it used to rank with the autumn Harvest Thanksgiving and New Year as a major celebration but when the nation became urbanized its importance diminished. Originally it was the day communities gathered to pray for good weather for the Spring farming and fishing, and included popular outdoor contests. The men would wrestle for a bull and the women swing on ropes for a more modest prize. Korean 'swingers' stood on the step or seat of the swing and the girl who swung highest was the winner.

The 'swinging' was said to come from the time when women were kept in seclusion, even in the countryside, and had few outside amusements. Swinging, besides being a mild form of exercise, gave them a chance to see over the yard wall and glimpse what was happening outside, especially when handsome young men were passing.

Our *Dano* day began with a lunch for sixty elderly people in the 'House of Love' in Pamgol. The women's group were at their best organizing a meal and by early morning they had large cauldrons of rice steaming over gas burners, heaps of vegetables being washed for fresh *kim-chi* and plates of the red pre-packed variety brought from their homes.

One team tended to the *bulgogi* grills, turning over thin slices of beef to make sure they would not be burnt. Everyone was in good humor, even those washing heaps of dishes and pots.

The old folk sat patiently at low tables, chatting quietly among themselves in anticipation. When the warm food was put before them they scolded the servers for preparing too much and too many expensive items, protesting that they were not used to being treated so royally.

There was much good natured banter as they began to taste the dishes and the men voiced their approval when I produced a huge bottle of *cheong-ju* spirits. I had received it as a present the previous New Year but had not opened it, not just for fear of what was within but because of its size. The elderly men had no such hesitation and many of the women only put up a token show of reluctance before emptying the glasses offered to them. The first part of the program was an undoubted success.

The second event was the revised traditional games that afternoon in Area B.

In the morning a 'farmers band' with gongs and flutes had marched through the alleys inviting the people to come down and join in the festivities opposite Pastor Kim's church. We had sought permission from the local primary school for the use of their yard but, after initially agreeing, they politely refused. They were afraid that the event might turn into an anti-government rally and the blame would fall on them.

The band consisted of the *Kyomunims* and a dozen high school students. Since the appropriate rural costumes were not available they wore colorful headbands as a token. When I got there I could hear their shrill music rising and falling as they moved among the houses on the hillside. Young children joined in, dancing, jumping and hugely enjoying the novelty.

By the time the band got back to the gathering point beside Pastor Kim's church a few hundred people had gathered and the narrow lanes were crowded. They were either quite young or elderly as most wage earners had to work even though it was a public holiday.

Of the traditional *Dano* program we had prepared all that remained was *yut-nori* and a lottery.

From the onset we recognized that wrestling for a bull and swinging high from a tree were impractical so the *Kyomunims* had proposed other traditional sports such as arm wrestling, top spinning, three-legged races (locally known as 'three-wheel-cycle races,') archery and a tug-of-war.

When we discovered we could not use the school yard most of those events had to be abandoned and we settled for *yut-nori,* the Korean version of 'Snakes-and-Ladders' on a community scale. It was more of a New Year custom but had the advantage of being easy to organize and since every child had played it from the age of three there was no need to explain the rules.

The games went on for the next three hours with loud cheers and rivalry that got hotter as time passed, attracting the curious from all parts of the hill. However no riots or anti-development demonstration broke out and everyone seemed to enjoy the afternoon's free entertainment. The police had a plain-clothes presence and the district authorities, thought they had not been invited to preside, were quietly supportive. The event did not solve any of the people's economic or housing problems but gave some pride back to the area.

***

While the people in Shillim 10 were fighting for their immediate future, downtown the students were fighting to save what they saw as Korea's soul. We had some university students in our community and we were located near Seoul National University campus so we could not help being involved.

Central to the struggle was the word *minjung*. Its English equivalent is 'the people' and for the students it had a deep significance.

They used the word to indicate those who had suffered throughout Korean history from Chinese and Japanese invasions, the Korean War and the division of the country, north and south. The students saw themselves as voices of the *minjung*, raising people's awareness of how they were being manipulated by America and big business, and organizing protests on behalf of the underdogs.

One of the methods of communicating with the *minjung* was through the *madang-guk*. In the old days troupes of itinerant actors went around the villages to entertain people with masked dances. These were held in the yard of a house or an open area in the village known as the *madang*. *Guk* is the word for a play so a *madang-guk* is 'a play in the courtyard.'

Under the Yi Dynasty the rural population had few opportunities to let off steam but the masked plays allowed them make fun, indirectly, of the local gentry and social hypocrites such as idle scholars and Buddhist monks. The audience participated in the singing and dancing and it was an opportunity for some social drinking.

The students used the *madang-guk* to remind people of their rural roots, giving them a Marxist interpretation. They developed the idea of *han*, the pent-up anger of an oppressed people, and directed it to a new cause. Poets and artists took it up and for a few years the concept of *han* attracted international interest. '*Minjung* Theology,' based on *han*, became fashionable and was taken very seriously by publications and colleges in the West.

In fact the *Minjung* movement could be seen as a Korean response to globalization, reasserting national identity in the face of Westernisation while highlighting social evils.

I was interested in the effort to articulate Korea's distinctiveness. The nation wanted new ways of viewing itself and the sacred but *Minjung* Theology did not seem to be the answer.

Around that time I was invited to the home of a lady from Haeng Dang Dong who had married and moved a short distance away. Her husband was a pharmaceutical student and ran a small pharmacy in his sister's name. Their home was a tiny room behind the shop and I went there looking forward to an enjoyable evening talking about Haeng Dang Dong and the people we knew in common.

It was my first time to meet her husband. I had heard he was an activist and that did not surprise me as his wife had also been socially conscious as a student. However, when we had sat down and begun sharing a bottle of *so-ju* wine, the husband began a passionate criticism of the government and America. Out of politeness I kept nodding in agreement until he started praising North Korea and said reunification of the country was the first priority. I could agree with that but when he made it clear that it should be unified under North Korean control I began to feel uncomfortable.

'How can you say that after what they did in the Korean War?' I countered.

'It was the Americans who started the war, the North Koreans were only protecting our motherland,' he retorted.

I turned to his wife, expecting her to support me but clearly she was just as convinced as he was. I tried to argue from historical facts but he said my version was all American propaganda as far as he was concerned. Now the *minjung* were learning the truth of what really happened and would no longer be happy until the American army left Korea, the government they were supporting was deposed and big business conglomerates abolished.

While I was sympathetic to much of his thinking, at that stage I realised it was time for me to remember that I had an important appointment elsewhere. I was sorry to see our friendship undermined but the young couple was not going to tolerate contrary opinions. I suppose I couldn't either but I was Korean enough to prefer to let each keep their own views than argue about it.

Among the radicals there were strong anti-American feelings and I wondered if indeed they were manipulated by North Korean propaganda or had the young generation their own reasons for developing that attitude.

Politics aside, I felt that what was lacking in *minjung* ideology with its anger and sense of past hurts was the wider Confucian compassion, or even Buddhist or Christian compassion. Change through violent revolution did not seem to be the solution.

The demonstrations were not single-issue and the motivating causes often overlapped each other. For people in our area it was redevelopment, for the Churches it was human rights and for students and workers it was *minjung* issues. Often we would meet at Shillim Crossroads, the transport hub for our area, on our way back from the 'demos.' The area was famous for its popular *sundae* sausage and anti-development demonstrators would share tables with student activists from nearby Seoul University.

Our Shillim 10 'action group' usually included the two ladies from the *aga-bang*, university students who taught in our Sunday School, young workers, Catherina Choi who took Columba's place in the Credit Union and her friend Lina. Lina was a straight-speaking young lady who worked for Pastor Kim though neither Pastor Kim nor the *Kyomunims* took part in demonstrations. One reason may have been that those gatherings often ended up as drinking sessions which would not have fitted in with Presbyterian or Buddhist practice. I would leave the gatherings as soon as Catherina and Lina began to move on to phase two at a different establishment, in accordance with Korean tradition of visiting five or more refreshment houses during the same evening.

I did not see many men from Shillim 10 at the demonstrations. It was not that they lacked strong political feelings but those with jobs had to be careful and, anyhow, demonstrations were for the young and not-yet-employed as they could go on non-stop for days, if not weeks.

In Pamgol we had our own 'community council,' like a parish council, that handled the finances and ran activities for the Catholic community. As in previous places, my living expenses came from the people. The president was a local secondary school teacher, a stout, affable man who was well able to manage a group that could at times be unruly.

The council meetings were usually on Saturday nights and if a serious dispute began between two members he would close proceedings immediately and say, 'Let's go for a drink.' I would retire for the night but the others would go off together.

At the early Mass next morning when I met the president's wife I would ask her when her husband got home that morning. 'Rather late,' she would reply but I knew that the problem would have been solved and they were all good friends again.

The men all worked hard during the week and had little time for entertainment. One of their favourite pastimes in early summer was to head up the hill to an informal outdoor restaurant run by a Catholic family which specialised in *posin-tang*, dog soup. Before the Olympics there was an effort to abolish this traditional summer meal but all it did was drive it underground or up the hillsides. Dog meat was considered good for regulating the blood in the sweltering heat of summer. Later, in China, I found that the practice there was to consume it in winter but with the same goal of combatting temperature fluctuations.

I was always invited along for the *posin-tang* and had to show my appreciation. It was usually served as a soup and the pepper-loving locals made it so spicy I might as well have being eating boot leather.

Shillim 10 was by no means the only area faced with demolition. The next valley, or ravine, beyond Area B was Shillim 12 and a very active Catholic lady named Sara was a District Councillor there. She often gave me good advice and invited me to one of their 'open days,' a song contest. I thought I was going as a discreet 'honoured guest' but was told on arrival that I was one of the judges and was called on unexpectedly at the end to summarise the criteria behind awarding the prizes. I was probably the most unqualified person there and had no idea what the criteria might be but my *choen-malsums* were duly applauded. They saw that I meant well and, after all, I was a neighbour.

***

By 1992 most of the problems relating to compensation in redevelopment areas were on their way to being solved through negotiation between the residents, owners, developers and city authorities. People were beginning to move out and house demolition began to create serious gaps in Area B.

Those who moved to another area saw it as an improvement. They had no deep attachment to the hills of Shillim 10 which were a temporary refuge till they got something better. What they would miss was the community spirit because they would be living in high-rise public housing where they were unlikely to know their neighbours. They all promised to come back again for the next communal activity but the number of such celebrations was likely to decrease also.

The number of Catholics had grown however and thousands of new people, with Catholics among them, were likely to come in when the middle-class apartments were built in place of the shacks. Seoul Archdiocese decided to make Shillim 10 an independent parish; until then it had been a semi-autonomous part of the main Shillim parish, near the crossroads.

I did not want to continue there if most of the original inhabitants left and a regular parish established with the bureaucracy and institutional responsibilities that involved. No other Columbans were interested in going there either so a Korean priest would take over. He was keen on maintaining the original spirit of 'The House of Love' and over the next few years he invited me to sports days and other celebrations so my break with the people and area would not be immediate.

As long as I was in Seoul I kept in touch with Shillim 10 and followed the local news. Some of the changes came slowly, even ten years later my old house and the 'House of Love' shed survived but were occupied by strangers. Down below the bus stop a five-storey parish structure had been built, with a church on top and a priest's residence, meeting halls and a kindergarten beneath it.

Part of the neighbouring areas of Shillim 9 and Shillim 12 had been incorporated into the new parish and the wealthier parishioners began to dominate the new parish council. The Korean priest in charge did his best to involve the Pamgol and Area B people but the demands of keeping a regular city parish happy limited what he could do. Julianna and some of the other old-timers are still around and always ready to hold a reunion.

I realised that it would be impossible to re-create a 'House of Love' elsewhere and it would be difficult to go back to traditional parish life again but I was already involved in some other developments and could now give them more time.

Chapter 12
'Stillness' and Tragedy

While working in Shillim 10 with the two Kyomunims my interest in Buddhism was reignited.

There were a number of Buddhist temples in the Kwanak hills behind us but the Shillim 10 people went there mainly to picnic. In the Seoul area, however, there were some important monasteries and I visited Hwagae-Sa where the noted Zen master, Venerable Seungsahn, lived.

The monastery was delightfully situated on a hillside, exactly where a Buddhist temple should be. A track from the park gate followed a rocky stream through the pine forest to an elaborate main gate. There was no entrance fee as this was a working, rather than a tourist, monastery. As usual, wooden images of fierce protective spirits occupied the inside of the gateway leading into the main courtyard.

To the left a four-storey building stood out because of its height and recent construction. Unlike the other buildings it was concrete, with three layers of colourful projecting eaves in Korean style.

I had arranged to meet one of the foreign monks there. Mark, locally known as Seung-mu, was American and had been brought up a Catholic but was now a disciple of the Venerable Seungsahn. He was in charge of the foreign monks studying at the monastery. A tall, thin man, aged about thirty, his shaven head and grey robes almost making him part of the scene.

I explained that I wanted to learn more about Buddhism and especially its influence on Korean life. Though I was familiar with the basic concepts of the doctrine and some of its meditation techniques, I realised my knowledge was quite academic.

Seung-mu seemed happy to have visitors. He showed me around the temple and said he could even get me an interview with the master. I protested that an impromptu meeting would be too much to expect from a busy person like Seungsahn but he replied that it would be possible.

The bottom floor of the new large building was a hall for worship and two local monks stood chanting before a massive Amida statue, with a visiting family bowed in prayer close behind.

We skirted the petitioners, took off our shoes and followed stairs at the back up to the top floor. The two intermediate floors were occupied by sleeping rooms and study halls for visiting foreign monks. The top storey, a loft directly under the sloping roof, was bright and airy. A long window on one side looked out on the pine woods and rocky hills.

Seung-mu explained that this was the meditation hall. I noted there were only six meditation mats laid out on the floor and wondered how all the monks managed to meditate there.

My guide stated that the local monks spend most of their time performing services for the people who come to pray for the dead, good health or whatever petition they had. Looking down we could see some of the smaller shrines where visitors were offering up incense with one of the monks.

They did most of their meditation during the annual hundred-day pilgrimage season which they spent going around to other monasteries, fasting, getting instruction from the abbots there and practicing Zen (or *Seon*, as they called it in Korean).

Seung-mu himself usually meditated for thirty minutes in the morning and thirty to forty in the evening. The rest of the day he was free to study or work.

It was already noon so Seung-mu brought me down to the kitchen in a nearby building. Beside it, under a plastic sheet awning, a number of monks and visitors were quietly having their lunch. The meal was vegetarian and Seung-mu served it, bringing the dishes from the kitchen on a tray. Included were various roots, mushrooms, greens, soup, rice and *kimchi*. Water and barley tea were available.

Seung-mu said the meal was free and open to all. It seemed the hospitality was not abused.

While we waited to meet the Master, I asked Seung-mu about the use of *hwadu*, words or phrases which help to concentrate the mind and remove distractions. Were they different from the Japanese Zen *koans*, paradoxical questions or statements that were meant to lead to spiritual understanding? He replied that, unlike the Japanese practice, the *hwadu* was to be repeated, not reflected on. The goal was to control the mind by removing consciousness.

Every day the monk asks himself, 'Who or what am I?' This is called 'the Big Doubt.' When you know the answer you are close to perfection.

After the meal we walked around the grounds and Seung-mu told me some of the temple's history.

It was first constructed in 1523 but, like many famous Korean temples, had been rebuilt many times. Once it had been a favourite with royalty but now was not as popular among locals. Under the present Master it had become an international center for Zen though the majority of the monks attached to it were Korean.

Finally we got to the cottage at the end of the compound where the Master lived. It was a typical Korean one-storey house and outside a jeep was waiting with its engine running. The Master was still inside talking with a group of visitors and I asked Seung-mu if the jeep was waiting for the guests.

'No,' he replied, 'The Master is going out to a meeting shortly and he will go in that jeep.'

'Does that mean he won't have time to see us?' I asked.

'Don't worry,' he assured me. 'If he said he will see you he will see, you no matter how long it takes.'

Shortly after that the sliding doors opened and the visitors prepared to depart. The Master did not appear but I could hear him apologizing that he had other guests to meet before he left for his meeting.

Seung-mu led me to the adjoining room and after a short pause opened the sliding door to the Master's room. He led the way in, bowing deeply and sitting reverently with folded knees to one side.

I sat on the floor opposite the Master and waited. The Master was sitting on a dais about six inches above the floor. He welcomed me in good English and seemed intent to continue the conversation in that language as he often traveled to the United States and Europe where he had his own centres and many disciples. However I replied in Korean as I wanted to hear firsthand the terminology he used. The Master accepted this in good grace.

The Master began by praising my Korean and asked me when I had come to his country (rather, 'our country.') When he learnt it was almost thirty years previously, he wanted to know why I had come and what did I want to get?

I considered this carefully and replied I had come looking for the truth. I thought it a safe answer and not incorrect either.

'Where do you expect to find the truth?' the Master enquired.

I was determined to respond as honestly as I could and said, 'Truth is not in books or the head but in the mind'.

'I see this is not a new topic for you,' said the Master. 'The truth is in the answer to the question, "Who am I?" and we have to study it carefully. There are many religions and they are all good but they are only ways and means of finding ourselves. The attitude must always be "Who am I?" It is only when we can answer this that we can digest who Buddha or Jesus is.'

The conversation became more general after that. We chatted on as if the Master had all the time in the world though I was aware of the jeep chugging away outside, impatient to get on the road. Finally I thought I should bring the meeting to an end and let the Master make his departure. Yet he seemed to be in no hurry and leisurely got up to see me out the door.

Seung-mu stayed with me as I made to leave the monastery. I could see he was delighted to have had the opportunity to spend time in the presence of the Master and listen to him. He asked me for my impressions. I replied that I was moved by the patience and calmness of the Master despite his other appointment.

'Did you notice his lips moving all the time?' asked Seung-mu.

I hadn't. 'All the time he was counting his beads and reciting his mantra,' he stated.

'Why did he do that?" I asked.

'Because he wanted to concentrate on you and nothing else,' replied Seung-mu.

I thanked Seung-mu for his time and hospitality and promised to visit him again. Later I brought visitors to meet him and he was just as gracious.

My own sympathy was more with Confucianism than Buddhism but after that meeting I began to wonder if Buddhism had influenced the Confucian 'perfect man's' sense of presence. While the Confucians rejected Buddhism, because they saw it as uninterested in social realities, they had a lot in common. The influence of Confucianism on the Korean character was obvious and I hoped to find out what effect Buddhism had.

Usually when I asked people their religion, the answer was either Christianity or Buddhism. If they said they were Buddhists it often meant they were not Christian but did not want to admit they had no particular religion, or that they were Shamanists or folk religionists. Confucianism is not regarded as a religion but saying they are Buddhists seemed to impress foreigners. Today 30% of Koreans are Christians.

Despite Buddhism's long history in Korea, I found that the majority of ordinary people knew little about its teachings, just as they don't know much about the formal teachings of Confucius. Yet every thought they had and everything they did is influenced by one if not both of those traditions. They have never reflected on it. It's the air they unconsciously breathe. In Ireland some of the best aspects of Christian practice have quietly survived in a similar manner thanks to the Gaelic language and customs. Perhaps it is there that efforts to renew the Irish spirit and society could begin.

In Korea many go to temple grounds on the big festivals for picnics, a few go regularly to worship and even among them only a small number would consider themselves Zen Buddhists. Koreans impressed me as 'people-people' rather than contemplatives. The type of Buddhism they are most familiar with is the Western Paradise School which looks for intercession through saint-like figures, public rituals and recitation of prayers.

Whenever I got a chance l would ask people with a pride in their culture, like Agnes in the *agabang,* about the influence Buddhism might have on their lives. It must affect their thinking especially in the areas of fate, *karma* and death. I had noted that when the Buddhist word for fate occurs in a conversation it is usually in the context of relationships, 'We were fated to meet. There is a bond between us.' When I questioned Agnes, who read a lot, about it she would not answer and if I persisted she would only get frustrated.

I was to keep up my interest in Buddhism and had an informative encounter with it in Thailand years later. However, while I could see elements of its influence on the people's thinking, it did not seem to affect their daily behavior to the extent that Confucianism did.

***

One of my other occupations while in Shillim 10 was setting up a Columban Lay Mission Program, the first of its kind in Korea.

I got the job shortly after moving to Pamgol, probably because I had encouraged others to initiate it when I was on the Central Council.

Along with Mary Ita O'Brien, a Columban Sister, I advertised for candidates, aged between twenty-two and thirty-five, active in their local community and willing to go abroad for three years. There were fifteen responses. We interviewed them and picked six candidates. They were all women. Columba of our Credit Union was one but I had known none of the others. We arranged a four-month preparatory course, including English language classes, and rented a house for them to get used to living together.

Following discussions with the Columbans in the Philippines we agreed to send the team there and their families gathered for a rousing sending ceremony in the Central House at which one of his auxiliary bishops represented Cardinal Stephen Kim.

I travelled with the team to Manila, the first ever group of Korean lay missionaries to go abroad. During the week I was with them there they settled into their house near the Columban formation centre and visited a number of possible work areas. First they would do six months of Tagalog, the national language and the one most widely spoken in the northern island of Luzon.

While I was there I did my best to help both the Columbans and the lay missionaries foresee some of the cultural problems that were bound to occur when a group of six Korean women became part of the Western-Philippine life style. The lay missionaries' English ability was not up to expressing their more complex concerns and no Columban in the Philippines spoke Korean or had an idea of Korean ways of communicating. However enthusiasm carried them along and I promised to return in six months to see how they were doing.

When I came back they had settled in well and were already actively involved. Two of them, Columba and Isidora Kim, had moved out to a *barrio* on the edge of Lake Laguna and lived in a house with a family. They didn't even have a room to themselves, all they had was a bed that was curtained off from the rest of the family room at night. They could cook in the house but were expected to be out during daylight even though at the beginning there was little for them to do in a village of just twenty houses.

At siesta time in the midday heat they retired to a watch-shelter in one of the fields. They had plans to build a one room *nipa* hut but had only got as far as collecting the materials. Their cheerfulness and optimism were infectious as they overcame new problems every day and looked for ways to get involved in the people's lives.

Their companions were also split up two-by-two, one pair in the slum area near downtown Malate where the Columbans had a church and the others out at a garbage dump an hour away.

The determination of the six women to be with the poor, and their ability to live with them, impressed both the local people and the Columbans. As word got out of their warmth and adaptability requests for Korean lay missionaries began to arrive from other countries. I liked to think that their attitude had something to do with the fact that I had interviewed them in Shillim 10. They certainly set a high standard for those who came after them.

Later we sent two more teams to the Philippines as well as a team each to Taiwan and to Fiji.

There were three members in the Fiji team but one left after a few months. The two who remained were good friends from school days, Yen-shin and Yen-han. Yen-shin was the leader even though she was younger and only twenty-three. She had been a university student activist and a veteran demonstrator. Before she joined she was a volunteer at a garbage dump north of Seoul, working among the rag-pickers and their families. Her English was quite good and learning Fijian was not urgent so they were soon involved in a program helping to create better relations between the Fijians and Indians who shared the islands but had a strained relationship.

They were there less than a year when I got a call saying Yen-shin was ill but not to tell her parents until there was some more definite news in case they got unnecessarily alarmed.

The next day another call came, telling me to contact her parents. Neither of them were Catholics and although I had met them twice I did not know them well. When I phoned them I tried to break the news gently but they immediately wanted to travel to Fiji. I said I would go with them.

Before we left the following day, I got further news that Yen-shin's situation was deteriorating, she had a form of hepatitis and though she was in a good hospital she was not recovering.

On the plane to Fiji I tried to let her parents know the situation was serious but they were so optimistic about getting her out on the next flight that I decided not to ruin their hopes.

Nandi Airport is about two hours from the capital, Suva, and one of our men, Dave Arms, met us with a car. Before we left the airport I took him aside and asked him how Yen-shin was. He said they feared the worst and that she might not be alive when we got to the hospital.

I broke this news gently to the parents when we were close to Suva and for the first time they had to face the possibility that Yen-shin might not be returning with them. We stopped off at the Columban house and heard there had been no change in her condition so we went on to the hospital with some confidence. Dave led us to the room where Yen-shin had been but she was not in the bed. Had she died? We were told she had been moved to the intensive ward and hurried there.

Yen-shin was lying on a bed amid a coil of tubes and Yen-han sat on a chair beside her looking distraught. Yen-shin's mother rushed to her daughter's side and saw her face light up in recognition. They were able to converse for a few minutes though Yen-shin could not say much. Then her father talked with her. When it came to my turn I think she knew who I was but at that stage she couldn't speak or move.

Yen-han had been with Yen-shin non-stop for the past two days and was exhausted so we all went to the nearby Lay Mission house for a break. When Yen-shin's parents returned to the hospital I went to the Columban house but joined them there later in the evening. Finally Ed Quinn, the local lay mission coordinator, and myself decided that the following day was likely to be busy so we should get some sleep.

About 2.00 am I heard the phone ringing and went down to get it. It was Ed with the news that Yen-shin had died. The date was 4 November 1994. I rushed down to the hospital with Dave but already the body had been moved to the morgue.

It took some time to persuade the parents to come back to the Lay Mission house. They must have been exhausted and Yen-han had to be carried into her room. Yen-shin's mother quietly disappeared into the bedroom but her father sat down on the floor of the living room and wanted to talk. I asked Ed if he had any whiskey and we put the bottle in the centre and passed our glasses around in the Korean fashion. It was dawn before we decided we needed some rest to prepare for the day ahead.

I was just into my second sleep when the phone rang again. The Korean community, mostly business men and their families, had gathered in the Lay Mission house. The Korean Ambassador was there and they were thinking of holding the funeral in the local Korean Protestant Church of which most of them were members. Ed wanted my help.

As soon as I got to the house I joined the circle, sitting on the floor with the ambassador in the place of honor. After a few words of introduction I mentioned that Cardinal Kim in Seoul would be sad to hear of Yen-shin's death. The ambassador, an ex-army man, of course knew of Cardinal Kim who had twice been named the most respected person in Korea. As soon as he heard the Cardinal might be involved there was no doubt that the funeral would be held in the Catholic church. With the help of their good connections in Suva the Columbans were able to organise a magnificent traditional ceremony.

Formal ritual is just as important to Fijians as it is to Koreans. Even welcoming an honoured visitor in proper style can take hours of speeches and exchanging cups of *kava* in the proper sequence. Lest a visitor make an embarrassing mistake, a local dignitary is delegated to speak in his or her name, making sure no disrespect is shown and all the rituals observed.

We had our first experience of Fijian culture that night when the pre-funeral ceremony was held in the parish hall. Yen-shin's father sat alone on the floor in the middle of the room, watching every detail and immediately at home in the solemnity of the occasion. One of the Columban students, a large young man with great dignity, acted as his representative and received the gifts offered, returning them with words of thanks, receiving them back when the offer was refused, and presenting them once more only to finally accept so much generosity with reluctance. This was repeated about twenty times. Among the gifts were expensive carpets to be used at the funeral. Two came from government ministers, both Catholics.

Yen-shin's father could not understand a word of what they were saying, nor could I, but he followed every detail with appreciation as only a Confucian gentleman could.

Meanwhile Yen-shin's mother sat beside me, subdued and watching. She had wanted to bring Yen-shin home even if it meant cremation.

'No one knows her here, no one will visit her grave,' she said.

When I told her the only cremation allowed in Fiji was Indian style, out in the open, she became reconciled to a burial and I assured her it would be in the Columban plot where there would be plenty of visitors.

The next day the church was packed for the funeral. The Korean Ambassador and all the Korean community were there, as were the two government ministers, an army general, the chief of police and many local parishioners. The Mass was in Fijian style with Frank Hoare, a Columban who was skilled in the local culture, leading it.

Ed Quinn, as the local Lay Mission coordinator, was supposed to give the homily but said he was afraid of breaking down in the middle of it and persuaded me to take his place. I did my best in both English and Korean, and when I told them of Yen-shin's mother's concern that no one would visit her daughter's grave, I added, 'She has just to look around her here today to be reassured that Yen-shin well never be forgotten and that there will always be someone thinking of her and visiting her grave.' At that stage I was having trouble continuing too.

It was a perfect blend of solemnity, emotion, celebration and hope. Yen-shin's family were deeply moved. We spent the next few days visiting the places where Yen-shin had worked and meeting her many friends. The Korean Ambassador invited us to lunch and we had a meal with the Korean community. An Indian lady heard of Yen-shin's story and booked us into first class for our flight back to Korea.

That was my last time in Fiji but Yen-shin's parents returned there every year on her anniversary. Her tragic death did not put a damper on the program, rather it seemed to have inspired more young people to come forward. The program is still running.

***

While I was in Shillim 10, every Thursday I would go to the Inculturation Centre in Wangsipni to prepare the next newsletter. This eight-page publication described developments in the very active world of religions in Korea, drawing directly from current local sources. I also wrote a monthly column, entitled 'From the Eye of the Missionary' for the Church's *City and Country Magazine* on events in Shillim 10 and after two years the editors of the magazine suggested that I put the essays together in book form.

It came out in 1993 in Korean under the title, *Return, O Spirit of Confucius!* There was a custom that when a person died, one of the family would climb onto the roof of the house, wave an item of the deceased's clothing and shout, 'Return, O Spirit.' In the book I noted, and lamented, the weakening of the Confucian spirit in Korea and looked for ways of prolonging its influence.

I viewed my articles in both the magazine and *The Korea Times* as a way of showing how Korean culture and the Christian heritage had much in common and how they might help support each other in a rapidly-changing world. It was one way, though small, of putting inculturation into practice.

During those years I also attended the meetings of the Catholic Inculturation Committee sponsored by the Korean bishops. It was basically an academic gathering. There were six meetings a year at which two experts in one of Korea's religion would present papers on aspects of that religion and how it might relate to Christianity. Then two other experts would give their response and finally the other participants would have time for questions or comments.

The presenters were all professors in top universities in Seoul and I was the only foreigner present. I would receive the papers at the beginning of the meeting and start searching through them frantically for something I could relate to as I knew I would be called on, out of politeness, for a comment.

The same tolerance was not extended to their own and I saw one lady professor's presentation torn to shreds in front of us all with no mercy. It was not so much that she was a woman, though there were very few women experts in that field, but she had done her studies abroad, in the United States. In their eyes she had taken the easy route to a PhD, avoiding the rigors and politics of the Korean system where the study of local religions and philosophy was more demanding. She was almost in tears as, one by one, her points were demolished.

I, on the other hand, was a harmless guest and a threat to no one. If anything I was welcome as a sign of international interest. Probably on the strength of my articles and attendance at those meetings, I was appointed to the Pontifical Council for Culture in the Vatican though in practice all it amounted to was participating in a meeting of 'Catholic Cultural Centres' in Chantilly, outside Paris. That gathering affirmed my perception that for European academics there is no serious culture outside Europe and no serious philosopher outside that continent either.

I stayed in Korea for another two years after leaving Shillim 10. The lay missionary program was going well and a team of five young people came from Ireland facing the daunting task of a year's language study just to get the basics.

The challenge of finding ways of introducing Christianity into Korea in a more natural, or Asian, manner remained but I recognised there were limits to what a foreigner, especially a Westerner, could do. It was a task for local people. Unlike them, I would never be able to speak of drawing on 'our' common heritage to develop a fresh spirituality, unless I was back in my own country, Ireland. But the country to which my attention was now turning was China.

Chapter 13
China Resident

In early February 1995 I was busy visiting our lay missionary teams in the Philippines and Taiwan and had no thought of ever leaving Korea.

In Manila, Columba was in an area named Elsie Garces, working with handicapped children. She lived up a narrow alleyway in a small room with peepholes in the walls gouged in from next door. Tina was based at the edge of a city rubbish dump where the smell was, for me, intolerable. There was no flowing water or electricity. She worked with the elderly who could not afford to move out.

Maria, the youngest of the group, had an airless room in a Malate slum from which she visited women in the area, many with very large families, introducing them to the services at the parish centre. Tersesa, small in stature but always bubbling with energy, worked in a drop-in centre for homeless children between the ages of seven and fourteen. I noticed a sign on the wall of the centre saying there were just four rules: no drugs, no fights, ask permission to join, help in the work.

The Korean lay missionaries were truly amazing in what they did and what they put up with yet when they got together there was no mention of this. They joked, laughed, sang and got enjoyment out of the simplest activities like going to an air-conditioned mall to see a movie.

When I asked them what they might be achieving there as foreigners they said they could help to raise consciousness of local needs, inspire and encourage their co-workers, help train leaders and expand their awareness of themselves and the world around them.

Like any group depending on each other for support, there were occasional tensions among themselves and misunderstandings with the Columbans who as Westerners did not fully understand the nuances of the Korean language and culture. However none of this seriously affected their work or relationships.

In Taiwan the inter-cultural problems were more complex. There the Korean missionaries had to learn Chinese which has a completely different grammatical approach from Korean. The people they worked with were not slum dwellers but lived at the edges of Taiwanese society: prisoners, drug addicts and immigrants. Being with them demanded more skills and language ability. Two Columban lay missionaries from the United States had arrived before them and were more advanced at Chinese. They could also chat more freely in English with the Columbans. This was an added strain but the Korean team kept up their optimism, determined to do their best and make their own unique contribution.

Between preparing new teams and continuing with the Inculturation Centre I probably would have stayed on in Korea except that events in Hong Kong and China started me thinking seriously about moving there.

As China opened up in the late 1980s Ned Kelly, our 'China Watcher' in Hong Kong, started developing contacts within the country, especially in the areas where the Columbans had worked in Hubei and Jiangxi provinces. He became a trusted friend of the controversial bishop of Shanghai, Jin Luxian, who almost single-handedly had got the Catholic Church in China back on its feet by opening a seminary, training schools, a printing press and new parishes in the key city of Shanghai.

One of Ned's projects was to organise gatherings or retreats for Columbans and others at Bishop Jin's seminary in Sheshan, followed by a tour of Hanyang in Hubei where the Columban founder, Edward Galvin, had lived and worked.

I went on one of those trips in 1992 during which Bishop Jin gave an optimistic talk about the future of the Church in China, saying that the greatest threat came, not from

Communism, but from materialism. I could see how much China had opened since Deng Xiaoping had taken over. When we visited Hubei University, near Hanyang, one of my confreres, Gerry Wilmsen, was teaching English there to a class of enthusiastic and appreciative students.

My explorations of Korean culture had led me to its roots in Chinese history and philosophy, and I soon became an admirer of Confucius. Korea remains the truest expression of a Confucian culture and I often wondered how the 'Scholars Teaching' was faring under Mao back in its motherland, China. The Columbans had also been founded as the 'Maynooth Mission to China' in 1918, so going back there 40 years after the last Columban had left seemed both a challenge and a duty. My interest began to increase.

After my visits to the lay missionaries in Manila and Taipei I felt it was time to make a decision. The previous November Ned Kelly had died suddenly at the age of 58. He was highly qualified in Chinese studies, with a Doctorate from Columbia, and there was no one with the same qualifications or interest in Chinese culture to succeed him. I thought my work in Confucianism might be a help.

It was not an easy choice but there were signs that what we had being doing in Korea for sixty years, setting up parish communities and providing needed services, might be coming to an end. Capable Korean priests and laity were taking over. Inculturation was focusing on academic research and opportunities for foreigners to do something concrete in that areas were diminishing. The lay mission program was established and could now take care of itself.

By May I had made up my mind and applied for a transfer to China. Almost immediately permission came through. Not everyone was happy. I had already left Shillim 10 but still had many friends there. I told them I was not going far away and would visit them often but we all realised it would be a major break.

There was no one to take over the Inculturation Centre and the newsletter had to be wound up, those who lamented its passing most were universities and institutes overseas who had used it a research resource.

The lay missionaries were disappointed as I had been their main link with the Columban Society from the start but they appreciated my decision to move on to a more non-Christian environment where the need was greater.

Once the decision was confirmed, the rush started. The small Columban China group based in Hong Kong decided I should begin with Chinese language studies on the mainland. It seemed like the ideal opportunity to get a feel of the country and I applied to Hubei University in Wuhan which I had visited during my China trip. Gerry Wilmsen was still teaching there and he helped with the paper work.

Back in Ireland I had to do the required medical tests and apply for a student visa which arrived just a week before the semester began. I flew to Hong Kong to see the people there and met a group of teachers from Ireland and the United States preparing to teach on the mainland under the sponsorship of AITECE, the organisation Ned Kelly had set up to introduce foreign teachers and experts to China.

Then, on 2nd September, a few days after my fifty-seventh birthday, I got on the daily China Southern charter flight to Wuhan.

From Korea I had been following China's opening up after Deng Xiaoping took over in the early 1980s amid the shambles left by Mao Zedong and the beginnings of a gradual and cautious re-engagement with the Western world.

A few months before I left Ireland on my way to China I watched an investigative program on the British Channel 4 entitled, 'Secret Asia: The Dying Rooms.' It reported that over a million girl children died in China each year from malnutrition and lack of care in orphanages. The harrowing scenes from a number of such institutions left the Chinese government embarrassed and very wary of foreign journalists for many years afterwards. The country still had to recover from Mao's excesses and social welfare programs had broken down almost completely.

Going into China always evoked a sense of apprehension, of entering the unchartered. This was not my first time but life there was still full of uncertainties with foreigners still regarded as either potential spies or exploitable wealthy tourists. Western visitors paid the highest rates in hotels and were charged three or four times more than locals to enter parks. There were rumours that their phones were tapped. Elderly men in Mao suits sat at the entrance of buildings where foreigners lived to monitor who went in and out. Westerners could not but be a little nervous.

The airport immigration officials in Wuhan were young men, dressed in military uniforms, very formal but polite. They consulted their computers carefully, took a few glances at me, maybe because of my age, and finally stamped my student visa.

Hubei University still had the structure of a Marxist Work Unit. The idea was excellent: people lived, received their education and health treatment, worked and spent their final hours all in the same place. It cut down on road traffic, there was no need to commute as everyone lived beside their job. A post office, schools, bath houses, shops and barbers were all available on site.

The most important Unit on campus was the canteen where all the workers (and all the staff were 'workers') had an 'iron rice bowl,' in other words, they were entitled to free meals as long as they lived there.

However the negative side of the Socialist system soon became obvious. Since everyone was guaranteed a job there was no incentive to work hard. In the post office the staff were usually gathered together in a corner drinking tea, chatting and ignoring the line of customers. Too bad if you were in a hurry. In shops there were no salespeople to help you when you wanted to price something or look for a larger size. When you paid the cashier, the change was likely to be thrown back at you as if it were dirty.

Later when shops were privatised, service improved and soon customers were as well treated as they would be in Hong Kong. By then everyone had learnt that 'it is good to be rich' and their business instinct, and basic helpfulness, re-emerged.

I was installed with the foreign teachers in a four-storey building on the edge of the campus, looking out over rice fields towards the 'Sandy Lake.' The ground floor apartment to which I was assigned was shared with a young Irish teacher, we had a room each but the dark kitchen, dining area and toilet at the rear were for common use. Fortunately Gerry Wilmsen lived two floors above and invited me to join him for his main meal which he cooked each day.

In the shift from strict Marxism to 'Socialism with Chinese Characteristics,' institutions like universities were encouraged to generate income and gradually detach themselves from dependence on the State. Education had been free under the old system but gradually tuition fees were being introduced. Opening a language school for foreigners was a possible source of new income.

The Chinese Language Institute at Hubei University had four students in two classes: a girl from Japan, a boy and girl from Queensland University and myself. The two Australians were in the advanced class as they had studied Chinese before coming while the Japanese girl and I were supposed to be beginners. Soon it became evident that the Japanese girl had prepared well beforehand and was no beginner so the classes were readjusted with my classmate being promoted and the Australian boy joining me.

Lessons were held in my living room but I did not mind as I had been living in worse conditions and at least I did not have to leave the house in bad weather.

Our teacher was a retired professor who used traditional methods, we memorised a page of text each evening and recited it in front of him the next day. Since the text was in Chinese characters it meant doing three things at the same time: learning to recognise the characters, pronouncing them correctly (four tones and two semi-tones} and understanding the grammar and meaning.

As the early Jesuit missionaries pointed out, it should be easy to learn Chinese as the grammar is simple: no cases, numbers, gender, time or mood. The basic sentence structure is similar to

English too: subject, verb and object. Yet it is almost as difficult as Korean because of the tones, at least four of them, each giving different meanings to the same basic sound. Also the number of written characters to be learnt by heart ranges from 5,000 up.

I had studied Chinese characters in Korea as they underpin Korean too, just as Latin and Greek are helpful in understanding English, but they can be quickly forgotten if not used regularly. Early on my teacher asked why I was studying Chinese, did I just want to speak and read it, or did I intend to teach it? If I was not going to teach I should settle for recognising the character and its meaning, not bothering with the writing which would take twice as much time. Each character has a fixed number of strokes and getting them right, and in the correct order, could be demanding. I was happy to settle for the easier route.

Every day we would have class from 9.00 to 11.00 am. Then I would take a stroll around the campus which was like a large village with domestic activities such as cooking and laundering performed outdoors. After that I would do an hour's study, have a light lunch, do two more hours class, take a walk outside the campus, return for supper with Jerry and do two more hours study. On weekend we would cycle downtown to hunt for imported goods in a number of shops Jerry had discovered. We cycled to Mass at Wuhan seminary on Sunday afternoons and afterwards I returned to study my text for the following day.

The professor was a hard task-master in the mornings when we had to recite our lesson but in the afternoon my fellow student took up the option of *wu-shu* martial arts so there were just the teacher and myself.

In the more relaxed atmosphere we chatted though our conversation was limited by my elementary Chinese and his lack of English. I would bring along my Korean dictionary and show him words relating to traditional practices or festivals which conveniently had the Chinese characters attached. The characters were in the old version but he would squint at them and say, 'Ah, yes. We used to have those customs but not anymore.'

He had witnessed the Cultural Revolution when Mao tried to abolish the Confucian heritage on the basis that it was feudalistic but he never talked about it. However he was impressed to hear that now Korea was more Confucian than China.

The professor asked me where I went for my walks in the afternoon and I thought it was just an idle question to stretch my conversational skills. I told him I usually went in the direction of the Sandy Lake. The next day I was on the causeway leading to the lake when two girls stopped me to know if I was British. Their English was quite good but they told me they had no foreign teacher because they were doing the three-year diploma course. They had to pay for their tuition since they had failed the entrance exam for the degree course and were excluded from certain classes.

As we walked along they told me about life on the campus and we promised to help each other with our language studies, they would practice their English with me and I would exercise my Chinese on them. It was only two months later that I discovered that one of the girls was a relative of the professor.

Both of them were from one child families, with their parents working in factories to support them, and they in turn would have to support their parents. Their English was remarkably good, far better than my Chinese, so most of our conversation was in English. I didn't mind as I was learning a lot about everyday life in China from them.

I had planned on spending a year studying the language in Wuhan but at the Columban annual meeting in Hong Kong during the Chinese New Year I was elected local coordinator and had to leave the mainland. The time spent there had provided me with a basic vocabulary and having spent most of my Saturdays walking up and down the alleys of Wuchang, Hankow and Hanyang (the three cities that made up Wuhan) I had lost any fears about travelling on the mainland. The local people were too busy with their own activities to bother me and the authorities let me alone once they realised I had no intention of breaking any of their laws.

We had been told very emphatically that there was religious freedom in China, that is, freedom to practice your religion privately. Because of the role played by missionaries in supporting the 'Unjust Treaties' forced on the Chinese people by the Europeans and Americans, no foreigner was allowed to preach or proselytise but I had no problem with that. We were free to attend the local church, in Wuchang seminary, and when people asked me about my religion I could tell them without going into further detail unless I knew them well.

The students I met, like my two friends at Sandy Lake, were smart and curious and spoke quite freely, within certain limits. To my surprise, they were more relaxed with foreigners than with other Chinese. Many young people at Hubei University wanted to join the Communist Party as it was the road to a safe job, like joining the civil service, and one way of getting in and advancing was to report on others. This put restraint on the old Confucian practice of trust among friends.

I attended a number of celebrations for students of Jerry who were accepted into the Party and I knew they were not necessarily doctrinaire believers. Afterwards I was to encounter some fine people among Party members, men and women with a sincere wish to serve their country.

***

Later my work was to bring me in closer touch with government officials but first I had a job to do in Hong Kong. From 1996 the Columban commitment to China increased. Besides myself, we had three men teaching in China and two living in Hong Kong but no permanent residence there. Now we had students from the Philippines coming to learn Chinese and experience life on the mainland so a base in Hong Kong became necessary.

Our headquarters back in Dublin suggested that we rent an apartment but unexpectedly money became available and we bought a large apartment on Waterloo Road, dividing it up to provide six bedrooms. The American Maryknoll Sisters provided us with an office in a building nearby that had been used as a clinic.

It took most of a year to find the size of apartment we wanted and to refurbish it. In the meantime I did a short course in Cantonese at the British Council and explored the city. It was still a British colony, the 'handover' would come later in 1997. A number of people closely connected with the British Government worried that the mainland police might have a file on them and were making preparations to leave.

Contrary to their expectations, after the handover Beijing did not interfere in the daily life or practices of people though behind the scenes, in politics and financial circles, allegiances were quick to change from London to the Chinese capital.

Most visitors to Hong Kong go there for the shopping and spend only two or three nights, seeing little beyond the mega-malls, street markets and restaurants. If they have time, and it is not too hot, they may cross the harbour by ferry or take the tram to Victoria Peak.

Yet 40% of Hong Kong Territory is national park and the hill walks around Saikung and Lantau equal those in any other part of the world. I soon got to know the various trails, the only disappointment being the increasing pollution created by the city itself and in nearby Guangdong, one of the industrial powerhouses of China.

Hong Kong can be deceptive. If the only people tourists meet are the touts and high pressure salesmen on Nathan Road they can get the wrong impression.

In busy Central, the profit motive unabashedly reigns. There is a standing joke that the temples to which people go to worship on a regular basis are the banks. They are indeed the most impressive buildings. Both rich and poor share an interest in the stock market, scanning the newspapers each day to check the rise and fall in prices. Hong Kong people say they need a daily dose of 'Vitamin M.' It took me a while to realise 'Vitamin M' was Money.

But there is another side. I found the majority of people outside Central remarkably laid-back, family-oriented and religiously-minded. While international business and education have Westernised them in many ways, the ordinary citizens remain enduringly Chinese and in no area is that more obvious than in religion.

There is scarcely a home or shop that does not have a well-tended family shrine. During the 'Month of Lost Souls' people burn incense and place fruit on the pavement outside their door for passing 'hungry spirits.' Festivals of local deities are major community occasions and thousands queue up at temples to seek a blessing at the lunar New Year. The police (and the Triads) offer annual service to Kwan Ti, the deity of courage and loyalty. No building or new enterprise is launched without a religious ritual beginning with a 'lion dance.'

Often when I had a few hours to spare I would go to the modern high rise 'new town' of Shatin, one of Hong Kong's modern residential suburbs. In a small Buddhist temple just off the main road, I would sit in the shade to watch young couples, or sometimes a young person on their own, coming to offer incense sticks before the many-handed Buddha. They did it so quietly and naturally that it added to the stillness of the scene.

Also in Shatin is the Che-gong Temple, a Taoist shrine famous for its warrior protector. At the big festivals, people queued up for a mile outside to make offerings and get their fortune told. Not far away a Buddhist funeral complex on a hillside is laid out on different levels, some so high up you need to use their escalator or tram to reach the urn niches there. With its colourful repositories and exotic offerings such as cardboard Mercedes cars, TV sets and computers, it could be a tourist attraction.

The people are so naturally religious and open to Western practices you would expect Christianity to have flourished in Hong Kong. The Catholic Church has been firmly established there since the colony was established and is the envy of other Asian Churches for its range of educational, medical and social services. Many top officials and professionals are graduates of Catholic schools and the majority of ordinary citizens have benefitted, sometime in their lives, from its hospitals, welfare

GUEST FROM THE WEST

programs and recreational facilities. The bishop at that time, Cardinal Joseph Zen, was widely admired and in 2002 was voted the city's 'Person of the Year' for his stand on democracy and social issues. The vast majority of the clergy, religious and lay leaders are local, many of them highly talented and experienced. Yet, in a city of some eight million people there are only 250,000 Catholics and the total number of Christians of all denominations is about 10%.

The problem is with the Church's Western practices and its distance from the religious thinking, experiences and approaches of the ordinary people. The Chinese, with their long and rich religious heritage, cannot accept a religion that does not resonate with their traditional worldview, morality and practices. This was to become obvious to me again when I encountered the religiosity of the people on the mainland.

Chapter 14
Managing on the Mainland

Although I was based in Hong Kong and lived there for sixteen years, the focus of my work was on the mainland. In 2000 I became the general manager of AITECE, the voluntary organisation that Ned Kelly and four other Hong Kong residents had set up in 1988 to avail of new opportunities for service in China. (AITECE stands for the Association for International Teaching, Educational and Curriculum Exchange. How that name evolved is a story too complex for here.)

AITECE was established after China re-opened but there was still little possibility of foreign missionaries being accepted on the mainland. Even among missionaries themselves there was a feeling that they should not go back in their former roles even if they could, it was time for the Chinese Church to take over responsibility for its future. Other openings existed. In 1988 the first four AITECE volunteers went to the mainland as English teachers and gradually the numbers built up to an average of forty a year. They came from Ireland, Australia, the United States, the United Kingdom, Canada and the Philippines.

The teachers were a diverse group: priests, Religious Sisters and Brothers, married couples and singles. They all had a primary degree and teaching experience and were aged between twenty and seventy. Some served for six months and others twelve years.

Their flights, accommodations and a monthly living allowance were paid by the Chinese government. Salaries were enough to cover their expenses though they wouldn't make anyone rich.

We held a five-day orientation in Hong Kong to prepare them for the change they would encounter. In explaining what we expected of them on the mainland, I told them that Westerners going to China were usually classified as one of three Ms:

Mercenaries, Misfits or Missionaries. We hoped they were not misfits and if they were mercenaries they would be disappointed in how much they could earn. Missionaries might not be popular, especially in China, but if they showed a missionary spirit of service, that would do. We warned them not to break any of China's laws and not to try to proselytise. The greatest challenge they would face was the culture and preparing them for that shock was a central concern of the orientation.

By the time I left over four hundred AITECE volunteers had been to the mainland, enjoyed themselves immensely and earned a good reputation for the organisation.

**

At the beginning the plan was to recruit volunteers in fields such as economics and industry but the most general need, and the greatest supply, was in the area of languages. The Chinese government recognised the importance of English in international business and even though basic grammar and vocabulary were taught in schools by competent local teachers, native speakers were needed to upgrade speaking and writing skills.

Education was one of China's top priorities. By 2010 there were six million students enrolled in 2,300 third-level institutes of which 1090 were universities. In comparison, the United States had 21 million students in 4,599 degree-granting institutes but the Chinese were just recovering from 50 years of education disruption and were determined to close the gap. Our teachers were at 40 universities in the north, south, east and west of the country. I was to visit them twice a year over the next fifteen years.

During my visits I was often asked, 'Why don't you become an English teacher yourself?'

The idea had appealed to me. The students were so outgoing and eager to learn they were a teacher's delight. Many of our volunteers had taught in their own countries and felt they had finally arrived in teachers' heaven. They found the enthusiasm and openness so appealing most of them wanted to stay on despite commitments to schools and families back home.

Once, when visiting our teachers at Sichuan International Studies University in Chongqing, a city with a mere forty million people in its metropolitan area, I took a walk around the fish pond near their residence as I waited for them to return from class. Immediately I was joined by a student, aged seventeen, wanting to practice his English. It seems he hung around the residence every morning hoping to meet a foreign teacher and chat with him or her on their way to the lecture halls. His English was excellent already despite having no foreign teacher. In his rural Sichuan village they had never even seen a Westerner and although he had a scholarship to study Japanese he wanted to build on the English he had picked up from the BBC to which he had been listening from the age of eight.

As we strolled around the pond for the next thirty minutes we discussed Irish and American literature and recent world events he had heard about on his radio. He was sorry to learn I would not be there again the following day and I regretted I would not have the chance to help him further beyond recommending him to our teachers. He had remarkable language ability and a determination to work in international business so he could support his parents. Due to the national one-child policy he was an only child.

What students like him needed most was speaking practice and the teachers helped by organising debates and discussions, as well as individual tuition. Those fortunate to teach literature were amazed at their students' imagination and insights, and their appreciation of what the teacher had to offer on a personal level.

A typical example from that time is the following evaluation of his foreign teacher made by a student in a northern university.

'I am very satisfied with your class and I find myself like a sponge because I absorbed knowledge just as a sponge does water. I think the essays helped me most for I was able to write thought-provoking passages for myself. That's true. I wrote for myself, not to fulfil your homework. Seldom do I make use of my own mind and the English language to serve my own action or thought but this semester I did. I want to discuss a lot of things with you because I think you can give me many suggestions and ideas with your sharp wisdom. You are a traveller of life who has seasoned everything, happiness and hard times, but we are still young students who know almost nothing about reality. You can provoke our thoughts.'

The students' eagerness to learn, and their respect for teachers, came from their economic and cultural background. They were the first generation to have emerged from extreme poverty with the possibility of endless opportunities through higher education. As the country developed rapidly there was an urgent need for professionals in business, engineering, communications, computer science and even law. But the Confucian tradition also influenced them. For centuries, to succeed meant rising in the civil service system with its roots in personal discipline. Generations had been taught that the goal of study was wisdom rather than an accumulation of knowledge. In the pragmatic world of Deng Xiaoping the emphasis now was on productive skills and scientific knowledge but deep in their psyche they saw education as a step toward personal growth and they were searching for personal examples of what it meant to be a 'complete person.'

I would not have minded being a teacher in that situation, and my interest in Asian cultures would probably have been a help. However I did not get the opportunity and the excuse I gave was, 'They say if you can't do something, you should teach it. And if you can't teach, you should teach teachers. In my case, I ended up managing them.'

Managing them meant keeping in touch with the robust expansion of Chinese education at that time.

In 2005 the government took a bold step in making higher education more available by doubling enrolment. Each institute took in twice the previous number of applicants and in four years the entire student body had multiplied by two. I could see the advance each year when I went there: new campuses, new academic buildings, new canteens, new libraries, new dormitories. Somehow qualified personnel were found to meet the new demands and the enlargement seemed to go quite smoothly. Whenever I had a meeting with staff members they would be rushing off again to prepare for another government inspection.

However, when I started my visits in 1996, the changes were only beginning and many of the institutes still had the 'work unit' atmosphere that I had experienced in Hubei University.

My first official trip was to Beijing, a low key affair that would give me a feel of the capital. The notorious 'Tiananmen Square Incident' had taken place seven years previously and the memory was still fresh. I approached that plaza in the heart of the capital with trepidation.

The square is so large people are said to have got lost in it, confused by its vast emptiness. However the Great Hall of the People, Mao's Mausoleum and the entrance to the Forbidden City, each representing a different era of China's history, provide landmarks. I could imagine the days when a million young people, waving their Little Red Books, gathered there regularly to wish Chairman Mao 10,000 years.

I was familiar with the royal palaces in Seoul which imitated those of the Forbidden City but the scale of the original was much greater. It was built in conformity with Confucians strict divisions according to role and gender. The Summer Palace, further out, was more relaxed with its lake and gardens but visitors were warned not to forget that this beautiful spot had once been vandalised by British and French forces during the Second Opium War. It was a disgrace which no Chinese should forget and avoiding the repeat of such a national humiliation was the duty of all patriots.

At the time of my first visit massive industrial development was taking place and Beijing as the political centre was first to reap the benefits. The people looked more contented, orderly and prosperous than their compatriots in Wuhan and Jiangxi. Unfortunately I had few opportunities to experience the daily life of citizens as I spent most of my time with officials and students.

The system of having a Communist Party Secretary as head of every factory and institute was beginning to change and gradually professional managers and educationists were taking on decision-making roles. However the Secretary was still very influential and he or she attended many of our meetings, though their Party role was rarely mentioned. I would often try to guess who the current office holder was.

I found many of the *waiban* or college Foreign Affairs officials more relaxed and open when on their own. Over the years I was to develop a close relationship with those who remained in the job and looked forward to visiting them once or twice a year. They provided me with free accommodation, took me and our teachers out for a meal and discussed the needs of the institute frankly.

Even in the Mao era, the Chinese diplomatic style was to welcome visitors warmly, show familiarity with their country, give them presents and so cultivate friends. However in many cases I could detect a degree of sincerity that might be absent in Western cultures where 'friendship' can have the life-span of a day. Sincerity was an important Confucian virtue and if mutual is still appreciated.

In Beijing my first visit was to the Culture and Language University. On the day I called, students of various nationalities were sitting outside in the sunshine playing chess. I could sympathise with those who were beginning their Chinese studies.

The university itself reflected the troubled history of Chinese education. Until the late 1980s all third level institutes were narrowly focussed, geared to producing technicians or experts to meet specific national demands in railways, power stations, hydraulics, mining and communications. Only recently had names such as the 'Iron and Ore University' changed to indicate the curriculum had expanded to include business, humanities, art and foreign studies.

The original role of the Culture and Language University was to give language training to diplomats and, to a lesser extent, journalists and businessmen going abroad. All were carefully supervised to ensure their ideological purity would not be diminished by this contact with the outside world. After Mao it soon expanded to accept a wider range of students, even foreigners wanting to study Chinese.

***

My visits to the universities brought me to different corners of China with an opportunity to sample the uneven development taking place, and also the culinary dishes of the various provinces. Nearly every trip also had a moment which brought me down to earth from a tourist's tendency to view the country through rose-tinted glasses.

The train from Baotou to Linhe takes seven hours and I had hoped that views of the Mongolian grassland would help pass the time. However there was not even a blade of grass on the low hills in that desolate part of Inner Mongolia and after an hour I gave up and returned to my book for entertainment. At least I had room to relax, the two seats opposite me and the seat beside me were empty. Then someone hesitantly moved into the seat in front of me, soon joined by another. They were two little girls, aged about ten, one with rosy cheeks and bright inquisitive eyes, the other paler and demure.

The first little girl shoved a plastic bag of sunflower seeds across the table to me. I hesitated and ventured, 'Xie-xie' ('Thanks,') the language student in me hoping I had the tones right. There had been few opportunities to build on my five months language studies in Wuhan. Her face brightened in response.

'You speak Chinese,' she said.

'A little,' I replied. I wondered if she was Mongolian or Han Chinese but could not be sure. I took a few of the seeds and cracked them open, leaving the hulls politely on the table though everyone around me was throwing them on the floor. An attendant came through occasionally to sweep them up.

She asked me if I were American and I told her I was Irish, though the name meant nothing to her. Obviously she was the talker, her friend just sat quietly beside her nibbling at the seeds. As we shared information on where we were going and coming from, her confidence grew and I was amazed that we were actually having a conversation in Chinese. I would have been too embarrassed to exchange that many words with an adult.

They were returning home with their families, who were just a few seats further down the carriage, to a town or village I had never heard of. She told me her name and her friend piped up with hers. I tried to repeat them but obviously got them wrong.

She next asked me, 'Do you have any friends?'

I considered for a moment and replied, 'Not here in China.'

With a big smile she responded, 'Then we will be your friends.'

She took an amulet on a red thread from around her neck and showed me her name on it. It was 'Dan-dan', meaning red. I recognised it from my Korean, even the pronunciation was similar.

She was delighted and insisted I take it. It was heart shaped, with a Buddha on one side and her name, with the words, 'Peace all your life.' She then nudged her friend who reluctantly took off a similar amulet and gave it to me. The name inscribed on it was 'Juan-juan,' meaning beautiful or graceful.

I searched my bag to see what I could give them in return but all I had were some oranges I was keeping for my lunch. They accepted them solemnly.

By then all the adults in the carriage had tuned into our conversation and once they realised I had a few words of Chinese they came over to occupy all the seats around me and ask what I was doing in China, how many members in my family, was I married, did I like China, how much I was paid and what were my favourite dishes.

My two little friends were soon pushed to one side and reluctantly returned to their parents' seats. After about thirty minutes they came back in an effort to claim their ownership of me but the adults remained in possession.

Finally the train slowed as it approach a station in the middle of nowhere. The two girls came to say good-bye and then Dan-dan said something I refused to grasp, 'Will you give us some money?' She saw my incomprehension and repeated her request.

The joy of the encounter faded. Delight at a display of natural goodness in children and ordinary people had been spoilt by the seeming opportunism of a relative or neighbour. It was not the first or last time for me to have a good experience tarnished but fortunately the good occasions far outweighed the set-backs.

***

Back in Hong Kong, in February 2003, a doctor from nearby Guangdong province checked into the Metropole Hotel, six doors up from the Columban apartment on Waterloo Road where I lived. He made his way to the ninth floor and infected nine people sharing the elevator with SARS (Severe Acute Respiratory Syndrome). He died the following day and the nine people, all on short visits to Hong Kong, went on their way spreading the virus to Canada, Singapore, Taiwan and Vietnam. A number of them also died within the next few days.

Immediately emergency procedures began with everyone wearing white cotton masks, the instalment of hand wash dispensers in every building and temperature checks at airports.

Fear of SARS spread rapidly on the mainland and many of the universities locked down, no one being allowed to go in or get out. Some organisations, including the Peace Corps, pulled their people out of China immediately. I used emails and phone calls to update our teachers on developments. While trying to provide them with the latest professional advice, I encouraged them to decide for themselves whether they would stay or not.

They all remained on, satisfied with the steps the government were taking to deal with the situation. One English couple who had gone home for their son's wedding even returned and had to go into quarantine on the campus. Later at a meeting with State officials in Shenzhen, the leader went out of his way to thank the organisations who remained.

Every year we had a meeting on the mainland organised by SAFEA, the State Administration for Foreign Experts Affairs. Originally it was just for the forty or so voluntary agencies registered with the government to inform us of changes in national policy and register us for another year. Later it became part of a much wider 'job fair' involving hundreds of international businesses and tens of thousands of visitors. Each of our voluntary organisations was given a display unit in the hall, free of charge, and we spent the day there meeting visitors.

The problem was that AITECE's supply of teachers was already committed to our regular institutes and I spent the time explaining why I was there even though I had no teachers to offer. We were interested in helping the remoter and poorer regions of China but couldn't send anyone there on their own or without previous experience in the country. As it was, we had people in Changchun in the far north, Inner Mongolia, Gansu and Xian to the west, Kunming on the southern border and Fuzhou in the east.

In the early days the government had a 'go West to the undeveloped regions' slogan with which we were happy to cooperate but in recent years requests were coming in for twenty or more teachers for language institutes in the big eastern cities. They promised us thousands of *yuan* per head and could not understand why we were not interested in the commercial opportunities.

At one point I calculated that all of our teachers were in contact with three to four hundred students each year, so the four hundred teachers we had over a ten year period would have met and interacted with about 160,000 students. Considering the great respect with which teachers, including foreign teachers, are held in China it was quite a contribution. I looked on it as our contribution to world peace. When efforts are made to stir up East-West antagonism, our teachers could talk of their good experience of Chinese and the students in China could relate their good impressions of their Western teachers.

Visiting the different regions of China over a fifteen-year period gave me a close up-view of the changes taking place.

In the late 1990s I visited Zunyi, a city in the inland Guizhou province that was famous for the picturesque karst hills that so often appear in Chinese paintings but also for its poverty. The town had played a role in Mao's Long March but there was little arable land among those scenic hills and foreigners rarely visited. Walking through the town with our teacher at the Medical College I was shocked at the distress. In the centre a crowd of young men and boys were sitting around, badly dressed, hungry looking and with nothing to do. We did not linger long.

Seven years later when I called in there again I found Zunyi transformed into a tourist city, mainly for Chinese, making the most of its revolutionary past. Its streets were bright, the buildings new and people seemed busy even if not prosperous. The change was due not just to the Tourist Board but to the mass movement of peasants (as they were still called) to the factories in the cities. Those millions of hardworking agricultural workers boosted industrial output but there was no state welfare system to help them if they got sick or lost their job. With no residential rights in the cities they could not send their children to the schools there. As a result, those who saved money sent it back home and towns like Zunyi blossomed.

Around that time I visited Kaiping, a city in the Pearl River delta not far from Hong Kong. When I told people I was going there they asked where it was. Since they had never heard of it I thought it must be quite small. However it is a growing metropolis of two million people, once known for its 'tower houses' built by rich South China merchants to protect their homes from bandits. Now twenty-storey high-rises block off any view of the 'tower houses' and the government shows little interest in protecting those monuments from a past era. The city is making a reputation for itself in the fields of textiles, garments and nonwoven cloth.

I missed the boat on the way back and had to take a bus which turned a four-hour journey by river into eight by road. It brought me over and back across the Pearl Delta on a highway that seemed to follow mountain peaks rather than river beds. At one point I could look down on a fortress that had protected Guangzhou (Canton) from Hong Kong gunboats and I felt as if I was peering down from an airplane rather than a bus on a bridge. The roads and rail systems in China grew at a phenomenal rate using the latest technology and were not delayed by claims for compensation or rights of way.

Most of my trips were to the large cities and towns where universities were located so I had few opportunities to explore traditional villages in the countryside. Any I saw had been rebuilt to attract tourists and lacked authenticity. In cities the 'old town' had often disappeared altogether and been replaced by featureless streets with the plastic shop fronts that had also been a part of the 'new Korea.'

The eastern megacities overnight became copies of Hong Kong, with even the same brand shops. Only those with a distinctive river or mountain in the centre managed to maintain a sense of character. The locals did not object however, they were happy to see the economy improving around them and even if they had to work hard to reap some of the benefits they believe their children would have a much better life.

I wondered how much this had changed the traditional mind-set of the people.

The older generation, to which my professor in Hubei University belonged, was still dignified and formal in *kunja* style despite Mao's war on Confucianism. Some still wore Mao caps and jackets, as if regretting the end of a time of certainties. Those in their forties and fifties were more Western in appearance and thinking, though they seldom offered an opinion that differed from the Party line, perhaps because their job depended on it. In Guizhou, when I enquired in the Poverty Alleviation Section of the provincial government as to where the poorest area was I got only vague answers. As soon as the official I had been questioning was called away, one of the women assistants approached and told me I would get nowhere with that generation, 'Keep up the work you are doing now with the young people,' she said. 'They will be more open to the concern you are showing.'

The young generation was open and interested in the outside world. They often amazed me with their knowledge of foreign literature, social movements and moral dilemmas. In fact they were more in touch with Western 'culture' than I from watching the latest movies and videos, pirated versions, and reading translated versions of popular Western books. Having being brought up with an atheistic education they were curious about religion and the role it played in forming values and life targets.

Still, the students were Chinese through and through and accepted the government's attitude that whatever was taken from other cultures should be adapted conditionally 'with Chinese characteristics' and that included technology, religion, art and politics. The Party could also depend on them for their patriotism, the only people allowed to criticise their country were themselves. As children of one-child families, they remained devoted to their parents and immediate relatives.

Naturally I was interested in their attitudes towards religion and, as often in China, the situation is quite complex.

When I was first shown a photo of an 'underground church' I couldn't help noticing it was almost two-storey high and standing out in a field. Not invisible even if 'underground.' The officially-recognised 'Patriotic Churches' are subject to the government's policy that religion be at the service of the Party and receive no interference from abroad. In response many Christian communities went 'underground,' refusing to accept the leadership of the government. Catholics wanted to remain loyal to the Pope and the Protestants were determined to protect their own independence though many kept in contact with their fellow-denominations overseas.

In practice most of the 'underground' Churches worked out a compromise with their local Religious Affairs Office to get necessary permissions for building and travel. They could also receive some financial assistance. The government is usually satisfied if the 'illegal church' keeps it informed of activities and does nothing to challenge the Party's political control.

It was not always that way.

Most of the older Christian clergy in China have stories of spending twenty or thirty years in confinement. That does not necessarily mean that they were locked up in a jail for the whole period, it could have been a mixture of prison, labour camp and restriction to a small area. One priest I know said he was made a 'guest of the State' at three different times for a total of thirty-three years while others were arrested only twice and did a mere twenty years. The arrests began back in 1952 and continued during purges like the Cultural Revolution. However those in prison during the Cultural Revolution considered themselves fortunate as they escaped the rough treatment suffered by those less well protected on the outside.

Many of those who were confined are still alive and living out their remaining years on the edge of retirement as country pastors. They have made their peace with the government, though they insist they are not part of the 'Patriotic Church,' and they are allowed a degree of freedom and support.

Yet a significant number of Christians, Catholics and Protestants, remain strongly opposed to the official Churches, holding religious ceremonies in private houses and running their own clandestine seminaries.

At the other extreme are the committed members of the 'Patriotic Church' who unconditionally accept the State's ultimate authority. Some of them hold high government office and have no hesitation in leading attacks on the Vatican.

One of the men who typified the dilemma of Christian leaders in China was Bishop Luxian Jin of Shanghai, whom Ned Kelly befriended. I met him on a number of occasions and was always impressed by his hospitality, ability to speak five languages, humility and achievements in restoring the Shanghai Church. He was imprisoned from 1955 until 1982 and on his release decided to cooperate with the government in order to get the Catholic Church back on its feet. When he was nominated bishop of Shanghai by the authorities in Beijing the Vatican refused to recognise his status but he earned people's respect by reopening Sheshan seminary, running training courses for Sisters and sending his young clergy abroad for a broader education. In his later years it was accepted that he was reunited with the Vatican.

Whenever I called on him at the cathedral in Shanghai, he would invite me to lunch and talk about his time in Ireland studying English. It was easy to forget that he was a busy bishop in a very complex situation. His ability to focus and give attention to the people he was with reminded me of the Buddhist master, Seungsahn, in Hwagae Temple in Seoul and Amalorpavadass in Bangalore. Talented men with presence and awareness, dedicated to their respective beliefs in completely different situations.

***

While almost all of the Catholic clergy were expelled or imprisoned during the revolutionary period, Religious Sisters were forced out of their convents, sent to work in a commune and encouraged to marry. As freedom dawned in the early 1980s those who survived began to search each other out and form small hidden communities.

In Wuhan there was one such group, a Congregation started by Bishop Galvin, co-founder of the Columbans. Ned Kelly discovered them when he visited the city in the 1980s. There were five of the original group still alive, then in their late 70s or early 80s. To help support their work he got looms from Ireland and an Irish Columban Sister to teach them the art of weaving.

I visited some of the old Columban areas with Ned and others to renew contact with the people there. They were delighted to see us coming back after forty years and even officials from the local Religious Affairs Bureau would welcome us with a meal. The Catholics recalled the names of the Columbans who had served there, what they did and who had been baptised by them. The loyalty of Chinese Christians was remarkable. Their religious identity was very important to them.

Despite Mao's best efforts religious beliefs remain alive even for those not affiliated with any particular creed.

After a SAFEA meeting in Ningbo we were offered a free trip to the nearby island of Putuo, famous for its statue of Guanyin and a Buddhist place of pilgrimage. Among the foreigners only a Mormon couple and myself availed of the opportunity and joined a large group of cadres who presumably were going for sightseeing and a late night celebration.

We had no sooner arrived on the island by boat than everyone suddenly disappeared except for the Mormon couple who eventually wandered off on their own. Not knowing where we were going to stay or what to do, I remained near the landing place. After about half an hour one of the officials, with whom I had been chatting during the journey, returned looking slightly abashed. I asked him where everyone had gone and he replied they were at the statute of Guanyin offering incense.

He saw the surprise on my face, what were Communist cadres doing at a Buddhist shrine?

'Well, times are difficult,' he said lamely. 'We use any help we can get.'

During my Wuhan days I was walking with my two friends near the Sandy Lake just after the Autumn Festival and saw smoke at the other side of the lake. I jokingly asked them if someone was celebrating with a barbeque. No, they said, they are offering incense and paper money to the spirits as this is the season when we look at the full moon, remember our families and thank our ancestors.

Over seventeen years I experienced the gradual opening-up of the country and a new pride in the people.

In comparison to Koreans and Japanese, the Chinese people appeared more confident with foreigners about themselves and their place in the wider world. They are aware of their four thousand years of civilisation though perhaps not of the details. Once the most powerful country in the world, they would soon regain that position through economic rather than military means. The vast majority were not in favour of war, it would ruin the economy, but they believed that from sheer effort and numbers they would soon be the leading financial power with the cultural influence that would bring. They had heard that students in the West were already busily enrolling in Chinese language classes. China would soon be restored to its eminence in the world.

Tim Connolly must have had an inkling of this when he said he looked forward to China's re-opening. The people are very down-to-earth and their heritage lies in practical ways of getting on well with each other and with the world around them. They leave no aspect of reality unexamined in their search for what is essential for human happiness. Even after fifty years of Historical Materialistic propaganda that inquisitiveness has not been narrowed.

In the early 2000s the government established religious research institutes in leading universities because they recognised that religion has, and always will, play a key role in human history. In recent years, ground-breaking seminars on the positive role of religion in society have been held in leading universities: 'Harmony and Integration of the Faith of Christianity in Contemporary Society,' in Renmin University, 'Christianity and the Dream of the Revival of the Chinese Nation,' in Zhejiang University and 'Science and Religion: Their Approaches and Methods,' in prestigious Tsinghua University.

Many of the top researchers acknowledged that they are impressed by Christian thinking and there is an academic group known as 'cultural Christians' who are drawn to Christian beliefs and values though they have not joined any particular church.

In China I never had the close personal relationships or sense of being at home that I had in Korea, probably because I did not speak the language fluently and spent less time there. However my visits gave me a respect for the people with their latent Confucian humanism and self-confidence. They do have much to offer the West, and much in common. People in both cultures seek a more humane society and while their approaches are different, that is how they can help balance each other.

***

2012 brought another turn in my journey. Our work in China was going well but the pioneering era was ending and I liked facing new challenges. A suggestion from Ireland to return as Executive Secretary of the Irish Missionary Union was tempting. It was an opportunity to take up what I had being doing there thirty-three years earlier, showing what missionaries have to offer both at home and abroad and clarifying why, in a greatly changed situation, missionaries still have their value. Society in Ireland had undergone its own revolution and returning there would be a genuine cultural challenge.

Chapter 15
Bringing the East to the West

When I returned to Ireland in 2012 I was asked, 'Do you find many changes?' I had being following events in the country in the media and through my visits back home but working with the IMU soon brought me face-to-face with the reality.

The IMU, for which I had worked 33 years previously, was now an umbrella group for 85 mission-sending organisations. Its day-to-day activities had not changed much. They included meetings on social issues at home and abroad, assisting returned missionaries, organising an annual program for mission talks in parishes and planning events to raise awareness of what missionaries were doing, such as a display unit at the National Ploughing Championships. There was also the follow-up on safeguarding children after the abuse scandals.

While I was immediately involved in the regular programs and getting to know people in leadership roles, I was conscious of two urgent challenges in the background waiting attention.

One went back to Tim Connelly's talk at the National Stadium: Have missionaries anything to take back to enrich their own country, especially from Asia? I felt I now had some idea of the answer, and the need for outside stimulus towards new thinking was obvious, but ways of making that exchange possible had to be found.

The second question had become more insistent over the previous ten-to-fifteen years and I had been trying to come to grips with it while still in Hong Kong: Was the missionary movement from Europe, and all it had to offer at home and away, finished for the foreseeable future?

The mind-broadening experiences of its missionaries overseas seemed to have had little impact on the Irish Church or society. Few missionaries felt a need to reflect deeply on what they had seen and done abroad or were trained to enrich their home Church with that experience on their return. Not long after coming back they found themselves conforming to local ways of thinking and acting, and the excitement they had once known became a fond memory.

The greatest number of Irish missionaries had gone to Africa and their contribution back home was in making the people aware of the urgent material, educational and health needs of that continent. It provided them with a systematic way of expressing their generosity and willingness to help. Supporting the missions preserved and cemented a tradition of sharing.

From the mid-1800s, dramatic reports of suffering and deprivation in Africa were listened to with sympathy in almost every Irish home and hearts were touched. Memories of the Irish Famine were still alive and adults and children alike responded with financial sacrifices. Thousands of young people also volunteered to go out as missionary priests, Brothers and Sisters, working in schools and hospitals as well as developing a parish system there on the lines with which they were most familiar.

Eventually the Irish government began to build on this tradition and channel famine relief and economic aid through the missionaries before ultimately setting up their own networks. NGOs also took over much of the fund-raising and sending of short-term volunteers in response to new needs in poverty-stricken countries.

The missionaries played a further role in highlighting the justice (or injustice) issues behind much of the famine, deforestation, wars and ecological disasters in Africa and elsewhere. This led to the growth in NGOs which specialised in international justice and fed into the increasing concern in Europe, America and the United Nations about the imbalance in use of natural resources.

However, any other impact on the behaviour and religion of Ireland is harder to discover. In recent years African theology, drawing on a deep sense of the Sacred, is finding its voice and missionaries have appreciated the joy and vitality of African liturgies but little of that has seeped back into the practice of the Irish Church.

While missionaries to Africa succeeded in raising awareness of the needs in developing countries, from the 1970s those who went to Latin America brought back the social message of Liberation Theology. In Ireland it caught the attention of people looking for a more actively expressed faith. Stories of Basic Christian Communities bringing the gospel message alive and encouraging people to work together for a more just society proved inspirational. However, while the ideas stimulated the thinking of small groups, in general the Latin America experience has been slow to take root in the Irish scene.

The Asian exposure has had even less impact. Despite a growing interest in Oriental religions in Ireland, William Johnston SJ was among the few to build on it. His books and talks on Zen made Eastern spiritualty approachable for many and I was one who benefitted from them. But Asia had more to offer than that.

My interest in Asian philosophy and religion had grown because of the obvious social influence of Confucianism on the people around me. The role played by Buddhism was not as evident but there were enough temples in each locality to raise my curiosity and my tentative explorations led to a greater interest in the inner self and what unites people everywhere. Taoism, though regarded as the 'third Asian creed,' was not prominent in Korea but I could see its role in art and the effects it had on people's attitude to nature. Shamanism, the great spirit-encounter of Korea, was fascinating in its similarities with ancient Celtic beliefs. Gradually my eyes were opened and I felt the need to know more.

In Hwa Yang Ni I soon realised that the people there saw the world differently from the narrow categories into which we in the West had confined it. One of the first articles I wrote for *The Korea Times* was about how my cook or *adjumoni* (aunt) viewed reality.

The column began, 'If I ask my *Ajumoni* why there are no towels in the house she will reply, "Yes, where did they all go to?" as if the towels had entered into a conspiracy against the two of us.

'At other times when she serves up the soup cold, she asks accusingly, "How come it is not hot? It was on the cooker long enough!" Besides being an admirable way of avoiding complaints it shows a rare respect for material objects, as though they had lives, and wills, of their own.'

Blaming an inanimate object, ghost or evil spirit for one's mistakes is still common even in the West. The habit remains in the language people use even though, if asked, many would consider the idea unscientific or superstitious. It was taken seriously by the practical Chinese however and they explained such phenomena in their own scientific terms.

For them, the principal life force is *ki,* the energy that people today are trying to tap into through Oriental practices such as Yoga, Tai-chi (or Great-*ki*), martial arts and mindfulness. It flows through the universe like the breeze but can be blocked locally by mountains and tall buildings. It also passes through people's veins where it can be restricted, causing illness. People and places who possess *ki* are healthy and prosper but this is never a permanent state, the energy moves between fullness and scarcity, between positivity (*yang*) and negativity (*yin*). The goal is to find harmony, a balance.

When I was in Shillim 10, I occasionally attended meetings of the local clergy. I arrived late at one gathering and found myself sitting beside a white-haired Korean priest. From the discussion in progress I discovered he was the pastor of Noriang Jin and I realised he must be the famous *feng shui* expert, Fr Lim. That science, called *chiri pung-su* in Korean, is the ability to trace the flow of *ki* in air and water. Recently he had written a book on his experiences and I had reviewed it for our *Inculturation* magazine.

His account was mainly about the ways he had helped people with health or money problems by checking the alignment and state of their ancestors' graves. If the grave had been damaged by water or the roots of a nearby tree, or was badly sited to catch *ki,* the soul of the ancestor would be unhappy and could inflict bad luck on the descendants. Such beliefs and practices are still common in Korea, China and even ultra-modern Hong Kong.

Real estate agents in Korea are called, 'Blessing and Virtue Room' men because they were thought to know the best locations for *ki* and it attendant good luck. Grave diggers specialised, not in opening the ground, but in aligning the coffin with the best flow of *ki*. I could accept much of this as we have water diviners in the West and making sure a house enjoys sunshine, avoids flood waters and is sheltered from strong winds is common sense. However I wondered how a Christian could accept that ancestors, who should now be in a more peaceful world, were bothered by the state of their grave to the extent of inflicting illness or misfortune on their descendants.

It was only later that I began to understand what Fr Lim was talking about.

The Chinese, and many other cultures, believe the individual has a number of souls. In the West, however, we have reduced the number to one, which seems to be an over-simplification of a very complex reality. When we stand at the grave of a relative or friend who died recently we feel a presence there, if there was no sense of a living presence our visit would have less meaning. Yet, as Christians we believe the soul has already left the body and, if that is true, the grave is empty. In fact our dualism has more to do with Platonism than the Bible.

Koreans (and Chinese) see it differently. There is a soul, called the *hun*, associated with the mind and the finer feelings, as opposed to animal instincts. It is the invisible self that leaves the body at death and goes to heaven or returns to its origins. When a person dies in Korea, the common expression is, 'He/ she has returned,' though they don't say were to. Someone who receives a sudden shock will exclaimed, '*hun natta,*' or 'my *hun* leaped.' The term is now used in translating the Christian word for soul. After death the *hun* is known as a *shin*, and is revered.

There is also the *paek* (*po*, in Chinese.) It is the physical or animal spirit, the conscious self that is attached to the body. After death it is called a *gwei* and takes on a dangerous or ghostly character. It lingers near the body, some say for three generations, before sinking into the earth. This is the spirit or ghost that can trouble the living.

Finally there is the ancestral soul. When a Confucian is asked what is his goal in life he will say it is to ensure the survival of his ancestral clan. Having children to carry on the family line is very important, not to have them is a crime against the ancestors. For a good Confucian, immortality means living on in the clan, the clan soul. Obviously it was difficult for them to understand why Catholic priests were celibate.

The question of souls almost derailed the progress of the Catholic Church in China. Matteo Ricci attempted to bring the Confucian and Christian traditions together by using Chinese religious terminology and adopting traditional practices such as the memorial services for the *'shin'* of ancestors. Other missionaries were not so understanding and, in their post-Reformation zeal for orthodoxy, insisted he teach the current body/soul doctrine of the Church and denounce the ancestral rites as superstitious. Finally the Emperor had enough of this foreign interference and expelled all missionaries except for a few Jesuits whom he retained out of friendship and to benefit from their Western skills and science. It took centuries for the Church to recover.

When I viewed Fr Lim's thinking from that point of view, it was more understandable. The soul that was unhappy with the state of the grave, and harmed the family for neglecting it, was the potentially dangerous *paek* or *gwei*. But the *hun*, or *shin*, had already gone on to its reward (or punishment) and was revered. The Western practice of leaving wreaths, or flowers, at the scene of a serious accident seems to reflect the same intuition.

It was not until 2013 that I discovered the notion of three souls is not confined to Asia, it is also strong in Africa. By chance I came across *The Primal Vision* by John V Taylor. I picked it up out of curiosity, thinking it was written by a famous anthropologist with a similar name. However the author was an Anglican priest-missionary in Africa seeking to find out how close the people's traditional thinking was to Christianity or how far from it.

He soon learnt there was an African belief in an individual soul, a life soul and an ancestral soul. The individual soul is like the Ego and lives on after death, similar to the Chinese *hun*. The life soul acts sub-consciously through feelings and instinctive reactions, it dies out after death, like the *paek*. Finally, the ancestral soul is received from the father and continues after death in the clan, in an underground world.

These similarities are a reminder of the complexity of the soul and how little we really know. It says something about Western religions that it is psychologists rather than theologians who continue to investigate its different functions. However the parallel thinking in different continents points to a once-shared vision of existence of which only traces remain today in the West. Taylor put it this way, 'By confining itself within the protective wall of the conscious and the rational the modern mind has left untouched the great deep of the subliminal, and unredeemed the glories of the elemental energies of man.'

Not surprisingly, the concept of 'life force' is as strong in Africa as in Asia. As Taylor wrote, quoting another author, 'The supreme happiness, the only kind of good fortune for the Bantu is the possession of the fullest vital potency. The worst adversity and, indeed, the only kind of misfortune is for him the diminution of this power. Every sickness, affliction or adversity, each injustice and every frustration is all regarded and described by the Bantu as a diminution of the vital force.'

Belief in the possibility of a more complex world than that taught by Western science today does not necessarily have to be seen as bound up with superstition, ghosts, souls temporally journeying outside the body or the influence of the stars on everyday life. It is a much needed recognition that reality is more multi-dimensional than we might think and that all living things, not just us, share something significant.

The Confucian scholars knew about, and acknowledged, 'other powers' but were reluctant to talk about them. They focussed on more immediate matters such as the challenge of building a healthy society. For them, the basic steps in achieving this had been clarified millennia before but since the situation kept changing, each generation had to do its own upgrading.

Perhaps it was because China took to a settled agricultural life at an early stage that living peacefully in communities became their speciality. The Confucian attitude was that if the family got on well together, the district lived in peace and eventually the nation would prosper. This family model was extended to local government and to the Emperor who was seen as 'Father' of the nation.

Even in post-Mao China, and in parts of Hong Kong, I came across villages known by a family name, like the 'Yu Family Village' or 'Chou Family Village.' There, within high walls, a large family or clan guarded its ancestral temple, honoured its living patriarch, held annual festivals and erected monuments to the famous scholar-graduates from its school. Daily rituals, as simple as greeting elders with a bow and offering incense to the ancestors, taught children how to respect and be respected.

The brightest students went on to take the national Confucian examination and if they passed were posted where they could use their talents and knowledge in making the country 'one happy family' though it was never as simple as that.

Memories of such unity and common purpose stayed with the young people after industrialisation enticed them to the cities. Their need to gather in groups and interact struck me when I got to know them in the growing suburbs of Hwa Yang Ni, Haeng Dang Dong and Shillim 10. Later I was to find the civility that comes from a tradition of living closely with others surviving even among Communist cadres in China.

The system can run into trouble in modern cities where there are no longer family bonds to hold people together. Neighbours next door could be from another province, have a different occupation and be too caught up in their own concerns to even introduce themselves. One solution was to affiliate with a church community and Seoul, for instance, became a city of church spires.

Many of the Protestant churches, in particular, started as very small congregations with only a few families and a service such as a kindergarten, but rapidly grew into mega-churches. The Yoido Full Gospel Church in Yoi Island, Seoul, began that way after the Korean War and now has a million members. Its congregation is the largest in the world but it still makes efforts to break the numbers down into manageable cells for personal contact and support.

While large church communities do provide mutual assistance and companionship they are seldom deeply involved in the wider society around them. Their members contribute to major charities but many may not experience direct social involvement. I could see this weakness in the first three parishes in which I worked but Shillim 10 was a model of what an effective community can do.

The focus of Shillim 10's 'House of Love' was on service to the people in the area. Beginning with 'meals on wheels,' it soon added a crèche, lunches for schoolchildren, medical, dental and gynaecology clinics, a credit union and events for the elderly. The benefits were there for everyone; religious affiliation was not necessary.

Ownership was in the hands of the people, local Catholics in this case. Activities were organised through the community council and even though there could be disagreements during planning sessions bad feelings were quickly mended and good humour restored.

People from other parts of the city were welcome to provide services such as the clinics, and their donations were gratefully accepted, but the local people remained in control. There was also good networking with neighbours like the Joseph Clinic at Shillim crossroads and the leaders of nearby 'moon villages.'

The bond that brought the people of the 'House' together was their faith and they gathered for liturgical services on Sundays. Although Korean Catholics expect the solemnity of Confucianism in their ritual they find room to express their joy and participation by singing. I have been at Masses with a congregation of only four or five who first had to go into a huddle to decide what five hymns they would sing with or without an organ.

Even though the liturgy was held in the areas used for clinics and other activities, beyond announcing upcoming events, the affairs of the community were not discussed at Mass time. Yet the presence of a Church representative living among the people was important. Everything, except the Mass, could carry on without me but I was the sign and upholder of what the community stood for and without such a symbolic figure the teamwork would probably have soon broken down.

Religious motivation also made cooperation possible with the local Presbyterian minister and the *Won* Buddhist monks. However it was never publicly emphasised. The outside volunteers were mainly Catholics, but not necessarily so, and the Italian volunteer, Angela, had no official role and was seen as just another helper.

A further positive feature was the fact that we owned no large or permanent buildings. Everything took place in homes, even mine, in the shed-like 'House of Love' chapel-cum-community centre, the crèche in Area B and the basement of a building near the bus stop. This encouraged informality, besides cutting down on expenses. People felt free to drop in and make themselves at home, bringing a watermelon to share in the summer or hot *ramyon* in the winter. As the lower parts of the district became more prosperous there was talk of building a proper church and centre but this was resisted until redevelopment was almost completed.

From the beginning I was caught up in the generosity, banter and informality that attracted visitors and kept the community together. It was what the people missed most when they moved to another area. It was what I too missed when I left.

The benefits of community are valued in other cultures besides the Asian but no one has studied human relationships and the balance of give-and-take like the Confucianists. For over three thousand years its scholars trained the young to show and receive due respect, accept mutual obligations and practice *Ren*, the compassion that should characterise everything. Today when people look towards the East for wisdom and inspiration, perhaps the people-centeredness of Confucianism has as much to offer as the person-centeredness of Buddhism.

***

Another area in which Asia has its own tradition is morality. Confucianists realised that for a society to operate in harmony its members must agree, at least in general terms, on what constitutes acceptable and unacceptable behaviour. In the West arguments over what is right and wrong are proving highly divisive and perhaps the difficulty could be avoided, as it is in some other cultures, rather by asking *when* it is right and *when* it is wrong to do something. The Orient, and Africa, take the approach that preserving human bonds is more important than defining the legality of actions.

When I was preparing Western teachers to go to China, I tried to make them aware of a seeming contradiction in Oriental behaviour. Often foreigners came with the impression that Asians are very liberal or lax in sexual matters but were in for a surprise. In fact Chinese, and Korean, society is quite puritanical. A foreign teacher may be reported for casually touching a girl on the shoulder or arm during class. It was Confucius who said that boys and girls should be separated from the age of seven.

I was never able to explain fully to newcomers why young Chinese seem so easy-going in some sexual matters but not in others. It was only when I read Taylor's experience in Africa that the explanation came to me.

The key to moral thinking is relationships. The relationship between older and younger, teacher and student and section head and staff members is special and should not be damaged by either party, especially the senior one, acting in an inappropriate way. This comes from the Confucian concept of *Yi*, or responsibility, mentioned already.

Even today in China, teachers *(laoshir)*, are highly regarded. Every teacher is looked on as a 'Master' or 'guru' and the student is their disciple for life. The respect and affection shown in return by young people can be misinterpreted by foreigners. Only when a person puts themselves outside the normal circle of trust, or formally enter a different sort of social relationship, are the moral barriers removed. It is not acts of touch or hugging that are wrong but their inappropriateness in certain relationship.

One of the classic debates among Chinese scholars concerned Confucius' sense of morality. The Duke of Sheh told him, 'Among us there are those who may be styled upright in their conduct; if their father stole a sheep they would bear witness to the fact.' Confucius replied, 'In our part of the country those who are upright are different. The father conceals the misconduct of the son and the son conceals the misconduct of the father. Uprightness is to be found in this.'

Years later, the neo-Confucianist Chao Chi commented, 'The great man sticks to what is right, which may not always require sincere words. An example is that a son may lie to conceal his father's stealing.' Sincerity was very important for Confucius but the bonds of relationship set the rules for morality.

Taylor claims that one of the points of deepest misunderstanding has been the Europeans' constant failure to recognise that in Africa the sinfulness of so-called sexual sins does not reside in the sexuality but in the destruction it can bring to relationships.

The lack of sensitivity in this area by foreigners, especially missionaries, caused problems when dealing with questions such as polygamy and people's sense of guilt. The Church's attitude to morality might benefit from a more relational approach and it would also be a useful starting point when raising social justice issues, both national and international.

It took me a while to accept, and I probably yet don't fully understand, the Asian attitudes to 'other beings', family relationships and morality. Taylor says they come from an emphasis on presence rather than mere existence. We in the West readily recognise the existence of others but rarely acknowledge their presence except by trying to avoid bumping into them on the street. The earlier, or Asian/African, attitude to others was expressed by a personal greeting. In Africa it is, 'I see you,' and in Asia, 'Did you have your breakfast?' In Ireland it was, 'May the saints be with you.'

In Korea and China the exposure I had to a wider thinking renewed my interest in my own Celtic heritage with its prayers and practices acknowledging God's activity in the world around us. Early Irish writers saw the sacred not only as existing but as present. Recovering that awareness could help solve some of the problems facing the West today.

Chapter 16
Future 'Guests'

When the IMU Centre moved to Pearse Street in 2013 we organised a display entitled, '1500 Years of Irish Mission.' The story of Irish missionary activity was divided into six eras with the final panel, the next phase, represented by a series of queries, 'Next, who will do what, where, how and ..... Why?'

Since then the topic has been discussed endlessly and three main issues always emerged: motivation, finances and openness.

Why is the urge to serve abroad in a religious cause no longer popular? What does it take to motivate a 'long-term guest'?

In general the Irish people, and even the media, are well disposed towards missionaries, often having friends or relatives among them. Reports of missionaries dying, imprisoned or expelled because of their stand in daunting circumstances have kept this positive image alive. Yet, for the last fifteen years there have been few if any new volunteers for the traditional life-long missionary commitment.

Some of the reasons are obvious. The institutional Church has lost much of its prestige and influence over what is now a more questioning public. Association with it is not as attractive as before. For the adventurous young, there are plenty of other options when it comes to offering their services abroad in a good cause.

There is also an assumption that the people of Asia, Africa and Latin America already have their own religions and, in a spirit of tolerance, should not be disturbed. Missionaries have not done a good job in explaining that this is not necessarily so. In most parts of the non-Christian world where there is no strong national religion, people show a genuine interest in hearing the Christian message and seeing what it has to offer.

When we went to Korea we were told it was a Buddhist nation but on arrival discovered that the layer of Buddhism was not very deep and soon so many people were joining the Church that we had trouble accommodating them. Today 30% of the Korean population, well-educated and comparatively prosperous, are Christian and the churches continue to expand. There, and even in China, a taxi driver would be only too happy to talk about religion and compare the various churches and temples with the same casualness as when talking about football teams or the weather. The freedom with which religion is discussed as a normal part of life is one of the pluses of working in Asia.

According to *The Telegraph* newspaper there are now 58 million Christians in China and the country is on course to having the largest Christian population in the world. The Communist Party is not too happy with this prospect as it fears Christianity will Westernise the country and promote liberal values.

While the situation in Europe look bleak, elsewhere the missionary spirit seems very much alive. The United States sends out the greatest number of missionaries: 127,000 out of 400,000 worldwide in 2010. I met many of those Americans in China, professionals engaged in teaching English or in business ventures so they can pass on their enthusiasm for the Christian message to the people they encounter. They might not all have the time or opportunity to become well-informed guests but there are over a dozen specialised institutes in the United States preparing them for the task while there are few, if any, such training centres in Europe.

When we sent our first six Korean lay missionaries to the Philippines in the early 1990s, we were proud of our pioneering effort but I soon discovered that 6,000 Protestant missionaries had gone from Korea to the Philippines that same year. Some of them went for a number of years, some for several months and others for just a few weeks.

One reason for the enthusiasm of Protestant missionaries is that their motivation is clear, and therefore stronger. They believe in a personal, direct relationship with God and a call to share this nearness with others. When they speak of 'church building' they are thinking in terms of communities of like-minded people, not institutions.

The goal of offering 'salvation from damnation' is still alive to different degrees among them and it continues to create a sense of urgency. At the same time, many are conscious that too much attention to the next world can distract from social involvement and lead to passive communities.

Catholics can be a little shocked at this enthusiasm. Their faith was traditionally mediated by the Church so, from the start, establishing the Church overseas was a major missionary goal. As I found in Korea, large institutions attract with their impressive buildings and greater resources but find it difficult to help individuals develop a personal faith. We compensated in the communities in which I worked by setting up groups or *huis* to support newly baptised adults in finding their feet and growing into their new identity.

How you see your role as 'guest' determines the motivation you need. If you go as a short-term guest, offering humanitarian service, it is enough to have a Christian concern for those in need, for one's neighbour.

If the purpose is to be part of a Church abroad which is in need of personnel or particular skills--to be a helpful guest in a temporary emergency--your existing faith and training should be enough to keep you going.

However to be a long-term guest with time to find out the hosts' deeper needs and help them develop in-depth solutions demands a greater commitment and more specialised preparation.

The openness of many Asians to Christianity is a fact but the present shape and thinking of the Christian Churches are very Western and give little consideration to the local religious heritage. Countries like China are proud of their long intellectual and spiritual history so the present enthusiasm for Christianity may not last long. University students I talked with on the mainland told me they admired the message but would not consider joining a Church themselves because they thought it too foreign.

That is where the challenge lies today. There are large areas of the globe which, for political or cultural reasons, were sealed off from outside influences until recently. A sizeable section of the world's population lives in China, Vietnam, Cambodia, Myanmar and the Indian subcontinent and they are now cautiously opening to other cultures and religions, to broadening their horizons and discovering whether they have missed out on anything. In most of these countries the nucleus of a local church already exist but needs strengthening and encouragement to become a more accepted part of the national conversation.

In countries such as China the role of non-national missionaries is not so much that of humanitarian service or bringing in converts but helping the existing believers to see their religious and cultural heritage as part of their Christian spirituality. This would help fulfil the promise of Confucianism, Buddhism, Taoism and even Shamanism and not be a case of introducing something completely new by rejecting the old.

Anyone involved in this task needs to be properly trained. In Korea one of the first people I encountered who was capable of viewing Korean culture from a sympathetic Christian perspective was Richard Rutt, then an Anglican priest in Taejon and later bishop of that diocese. Before going to Korea he had studied in Cambridge as had John V Taylor whose book *The Primal Vision* I was to read with much benefit many years later. Both were pioneers in the study of local cultures and world views, and the liberal education they received in Cambridge must have helped prepare them for the challenge.

Unfortunately the training of most Catholic missionaries like myself was limited to Western theology, Church Law and spirituality with little thought that these might have to be re-interpreted to suit non-European mind-sets in Asia and Africa. There was a conviction that the Roman, and European, model suited all cultures and that outlook was passed on in the training of local Church leaders with the result that many still consider it their duty to preserve what the missionaries gave them.

Then there is the difficult area of finances.

Most of the Protestant missionaries I met in Asia were married and some even had their children with them. They received material support from their Fellowship or parish community back home which had a mission budget and paid the missionaries' expenses through one of the large mission-sending organisations.

The Catholic system is different. Until recently, long-term missionaries like myself were priests or members of Religious Congregations who had a support system in their home Church. However there was no tradition of financing lay people in the same manner. Existing lay groups, largely run by volunteers, have trouble providing their people in the field with a living allowance, insurance and a resettlement fund. They would be seriously limited in the number of people they send if it were not for their involvement in government-funded projects. Yet, as most of these programs have strictly secular objectives they limit opportunities to participate in religious activities with the local people.

At present mission-related lay groups in Ireland are beginning to come together to discuss their status and plan cooperation in taking the next step forward. As the Irish Church changes and becomes more involved in building communities led by the laity, financing lay mission should be less of a problem.

However, even when there is a long-term commitment, and sufficient financial support is provided, not everyone is suited for life as a long-term international 'guest.' An inability to deal with culture shock in one symptom and we had new teachers in China who demanded to be returned home immediately after just one day of being reduced to childhood helplessness by an inability to speak the language or go out unaccompanied. Most of them did get over it and survived to enjoy the rest of their stay but a number had to accept that life in a completely different culture was too great a challenge for them.

Those who remain abroad for many years and get deeply immersed in local life face another form of identity crisis.

Two of the greatest compliments I ever received came from the son of our area leader in Kun-ja District, Hwa Yang Ni. The first time his mother brought him, around age six, to the church he came up to me after Mass, bowed and said, 'God, How is your health?' His mother must have told him he was in God's house and as I seemed to be the person in charge, he presumed I was God.

His mother probably straightened him out on that but about a year later he approached me again and said, 'Father, you are a Korean, aren't you?' Remembering that Confucius said it was OK to bend the truth to preserve relationships, I replied, 'Yes, of course I am.'

Those two incidents made me reflect on the position of foreigners in Korea, neither fish nor flesh, and I wrote an article on the topic for *The Korea Times*.

I said, 'Most Westerners in Korea are here for only a short time so they get to know very little of the language and culture. As a result they live in an isolated world, will be treated politely by the few locals they are introduced to but will be regarded as fair game by the majority. However those who learn Korean soon experience its miraculous effects. A few words in the language of the country will turn a group of curious villagers, loudly discussing among themselves the peculiarities of the foreigner, into polite and friendly (though slightly abashed) individuals prepared to treat you as a long-absent relative. The few words will likewise make unpleasant characters disappear and ensure fair play from shop men and taxi drivers.

'A little knowledge of the culture and a little empathy will be even more rewarding. In fact you may be so overcome by the enthusiasm with which you are received that for one fatal moment you think that you have arrived, that you are accepted as an equal, as a Korean. But things are not that simple.

'People who have spent decades in Korea, who know the country, its language, its culture and peculiarities as well as most of the locals, find themselves being constantly reminded that they are foreigners. In the area in which they live they might be well known and greeted in Korean wherever they go but sooner or later a stranger is going to appear who addresses them in English and has to go through the whole process again: "When did you come to Korea? What is your home county? Where is your family?" and so on. You are reminded that you are an outsider.

'Not only that, there are occasions when those who have accepted you as a friend seem to treat you with a double standard. They expect you to act as a Korean but treat you as a foreigner. As one colleague put it, "When a local uses the polite expression, 'Please counsel me well,' to a fellow Korean whom he meets for the first time, the other party would know better than to take him seriously, but if a foreigner uses the same words the guy will be back that night to take him up on it."

'However in Korea the benefits of knowing the language and culture are so great, so many doors are opened to you, that you are tempted to feel you are accepted one hundred percent. There are so many understanding and helpful people around that the rude shocks that remind you that you are very much a foreigner are all the more painful when they come.

'But if you only think of that aspect of living in Korea you will miss much of what is truly unique in this country. And the other side is well worth discovering.'

I was one of those who stayed on and was content to see myself as a welcomed guest. However when I reflect on how much I have been changed by my life in Asia, I have to admit that I was never in danger of completely becoming an Asian. My Western background was too deeply ingrained.

The importance of individualism and personal freedom was so imbedded in my thinking that any transformation was slow and, sadly, incomplete. While I had great admiration for the Confucian 'Perfect Person' I never succeed in becoming one.

For instance, in Korea I was regarded as a 'Spiritual Father' (*Shin-bu-nim*) and expected never to forget it. In most of Asia people are addressed by a title associated with their role in society rather than their name. 'Older brother' and 'older sister' are terms used among friends who are not even related, 'Aunt' and 'Uncle' apply to middle-aged people you meet on the street, 'Grandfather' is any man over sixty and a *huijang* could be the head of any group from a school club to a conglomerate. Only seniors can address juniors they know by their personal name. It is a great reminder of who you are to the people you meet and how you are expected to behave.

The Korean language and even modern Chinese have dozens of precise terms for such roles and relationships. When I went on trips to China from Hong Kong I told Rita, my Chinese assistant for twelve years, to be careful about using religious titles and never to use the word 'Father' in messages she sent to me on the mainland. Her only solution was to use initials, 'F. Hugh.'

Until recently most cultures knew that formality but now in the West the only professional titles regularly used are 'Doctor,' 'Nurse' and 'Judge.' Politicians and clergy are more commonly addressed by their Christian names, which would be unthinkable in Asia.

When chatting with young people I would be caught between the desire to use informal language and the cultural demand to address them in a rigid and solemn manner. It was difficult, if not impossible, to just 'be myself.'

Similarly, in talks and formal presentations there was no room for light humour unless I began with, 'What I am about to say next is a joke.' Then everyone would dutifully laugh. Esteemed people say only serious things and should be listened to solemnly. With such expectations it is difficult to put people at their ease or be relaxed with them.

These are just some examples of how Eastern practices challenge the informality and equality with which Westerners are accustomed. Yet, despite my preference to be seen as a fellow-human rather than a remote role-figure, I can appreciate what Confucius taught. He said, 'There is effective society only when the ruler is ruler, when the minister is minister, when the father is father and the son is son.' A more modern version is, 'Children have many friends in life but only one person can be their father or mother.' I could accept the need to take responsibility for what I meant to others but it often meant distancing myself from them.

My interest in Buddhism also revealed my human limitations. Buddhism teaches the importance of the present moment, the only one we live in, and of not depending on material things. Despite my admiration for this attitude to life, I am still impatient to think about what might happen next and to want things that might make the future better. Buddhism has valuable lessons in cultivating an inner life but the cost is strict self-discipline and a willingness to reject all external attractions.

Taoism advises people to relax and 'go with the flow of nature.' Such a 'drop-out-of-society' attitude was popular in the West in the 1960s and its Oriental version attracted me but my inclination to achieve something and improve on nature remains.

When it comes to ghosts, spirits and other-world-forces not yet understood by Western science, Korean Shamanism has broadened my outlook. It embraces a view of life that goes back to the earliest humans and has been preserved in many cultures, including my own Celtic heritage, giving life a freshness and openness to possibilities that would be sadly missed. However, I am in no hurry to initiate direct contact with the fourth dimension.

For those reasons I can't say I am a completely different person because of my Asian encounters, but I am now more aware that there are alternatives. When I feel I might be going too far in the rational, egocentric and material direction, some of what I was exposed to in Korea and China kicks in, reminding me that I am in danger of being swallowed up in a too-narrow world. Asia can't change the direction the West has taken but might just broaden its imagination and what it thinks is important.

Overall, my ideas on relationships, morality and a wider presence in the world have definitely been upgraded. I hope the people I encountered on the way got something from me in return.

Postscript

Today, with improved travel and media, more Westerners than ever are visiting China and more Chinese coming to the West. There are now over 430 'Confucian Institutes' worldwide, sponsored by the Chinese Government, teaching the Chinese language to non-Chinese. If ever there was a time when Tim Connolly's prediction that China can contribute to the well-being of the West might be fulfilled, this could be the moment.

Asia offers the West an alternative approach to life issues and it will be interesting to see how much the social intuitions of Confucianism, the inner search of Buddhism, Taoist reflection on nature and the Shamanistic world of spirits are able to modify the West's sense of social and economic priorities.

Western theological thinking needs to be challenged but only Asians themselves, when they have the confidence and encouragement to do so, can adequately describe what they have to offer. When they do so, they will provide fresh attitudes to reality, creation, human existence, suffering and death. Already their voice is beginning to be heard, in China of all places, where prestigious universities debate how Christianity and Confucianism can help balance each other. However, whatever Asia brings will not be dualistic, it will not be based on clear distinctions between sacred and worldly realities, body and soul, good and bad, us and them.

I never did became fully Asian in my thinking and behaviour but my steps in that direction led me to discover (or re-discover?) my own Celtic heritage and its distinctive way of drawing on, and expressing, a sense of presence in the world. It is that which unites people everywhere with others, nature and the Creator. If it takes exposure to a different culture to make one aware of the treasures in one's own, then long-term 'guests' should be a valuable resource.

How would the US sergeant, who asked me what was I doing in Korea back in 1964, think of the response that I wanted to bring back to the West some of what it had lost in its materialistic approach to human development? He would have thought I was out in the sun too long and I wouldn't blame him. At that time I was not that advanced in my thinking either, what I too was looking for was something more immediate and compelling. My thoughts were on the lines of what I had to give rather than what I could receive and indeed I would never have started out on my journey if I had not felt I had some gift to bring with me.

The challenge of expressing what motivated me in language that was both accurate and clear cropped up again when I worked for the IMU in 1979 and when I returned to the new Ireland in 2012. No catchy slogan had emerged that would make modern missionary work instantly intelligible to people.

A number of possible answers have come to me over the years. The idea of helping to create a world of 'justice, peace and love,' the 'Reign of God' that Jesus represented, is still attractive just as it was in the '70s and '80s. The more I got to appreciate Oriental religions however, I found the idea of 'fullness', of fulfilling the people's deepest aspirations, closer to the heart of the matter.

Helping to bring the 'Good News' message across cultural barriers to have it enrich other religious traditions, and in doing so have your own understandings deepened, sounds demanding but is worth the effort.

Maybe the Korean Lay Missionaries in the Philippines put it best when they told me one of the reasons they were there was to 'expand the awareness of themselves and the world around them.' It reminded me of the Buddhist Master in Seoul saying it was a search for an answer to, 'Who am I?'

What would the older generation of missionaries think of this? They were the ones who set up parishes, communities and services in Asia, Africa and Latin America when they were most needed. They were trained for that work only and they put all their energy into it, using limited resources with ingenuity and staying on when it was unsafe. The personal impact they made on people all over the world is probably their greatest contribution.

Now they are leaving to others the task of helping the young Churches in Africa, Asia and Latin America draw more on their own heritage and deepen their roots in traditional culture. This, in turn, will enable countries like China to make the contribution that Tim Connolly looked forward to: bringing a fresh understanding and practice of the Christian message to a world in need of revitalisation.

The search continues and hopefully the tradition of wanting to live as a guest in another culture, sharing what you believe with the people there, and being open to learning from them, will last.